THE

LIFE AND TIMES

OF AN

INVOLUNTARY

GENIUS

BY ANDREI CODRESCU

License to Carry a Gun

A Serious Morning

The History of the Growth of Heaven

THE
Life and Times
OF AN
Involuntary
Genius

ANDREI CODRESCU

A VENTURE BOOK

George Braziller   New York

The Author wishes to thank
the National Endowment for the Arts
for a grant which gave him the time.

Many thanks also to Michael & Karen
Braziller for their patience.

The Salvador Dali quote
is from *Diary of a Genius* (Doubleday 1965).

Published simultaneously in Canada by
Doubleday, Canada Limited.
All rights reserved.

For information, address the publisher:
George Braziller, Inc.
One Park Avenue, New York 10016

International Standard Book Number: 0–8076–0773–8
Library of Congress Catalog Card Number: 74–24906

First Printing

Printed in the United States of America

For Alice,
          who knew what it was
          when it wasn't
&
for Lucian,
          who does it
&
yes, for mother

And if in our age of quasi-dwarfs the colossal scandal of being a genius permits us not to be stoned like dogs or to starve to death, it will only be by the grace of God.

—Salvador Dali

Sears credit furniture surrounded Mother, and a reproduction of a Sears field of yellow flowers with something red in the sky hovered over her. Her new couches were still covered by the factory plastic and, with infinite protection, seemed to be on their way to immortality. This original plastic was also on the inside of her car which she learned to drive at the age of forty-six. She drove it to the factory for two hours and then she drove it back for two more. On the dashboard was a rabbit's foot and a brown bear.

She had grown so old. He didn't know how young or how old mothers stay in children's heads, but his mother had been young in his and now she was old. Having been beautiful in her youth and even later on, she had always tried to pass him off as her brother rather than her son. In fact, whenever she used to say that he was her son, the other folks would immediately begin to shake their heads and say: "No, no, that's not your son. That's your brother." And they would wink to each other. Her face had acquired a new set of lines which made little buildings in various pudgy sections so that she now had a city around her nose, her mouth and her eyebrows.

It was an affectionate meeting. She kissed everybody millions of times and, all the while, she gave her son looks mixed with sweetness and reproach. Her reproach was directed to things he hadn't thought about in years. Reproach for not continuing his studies. For not being a doctor. For leaving her. For not writing. For not calling. For being weird. For having long hair. For wearing those kinds of shoes. Old and forgotten things, in general, but things which had stayed with her. The sweetness, on the other hand, was both a support for the reproach and something all its own, a sort of warm chamber in a dim and comfortable prehistory.

–But four years, mother was saying, four years is an eternity . . . What did you do?

–Oh this and that. . . .

He had forgotten the way she used to have her reality censored —he didn't want to shock her.

–New York was too much and California was the promised land . . . We went there. We were on welfare in San Francisco.

–Weren't you ashamed? Thank God, mother and the family don't know anything about this. I wrote them that you were a big writer.

–From San Francisco we moved to the country. . . .

Mother picked up his son Lucian and smothered him with kisses. Lucian was overwhelmed. Something beyond his understanding was going on. He'd been very shy ever since they arrived.

–Grandma will take good care of you.

–In San Francisco I gave a lot of poetry readings. . . .

–Did they pay well?

–Not too well. Enough to eat and stuff.

–What are you eating?

–All kinds of things, said his wife Alice. Steaks and broccoli, fish, vegetables . . . the vegetables are very fresh in California.

–Do you drink milk?

–Sure.

Mother grabbed Lucian and looked him over, worried.

–Would you like a little milk, sweetheart?

–No, said Lucian.

She tried to feed them the whole time. She had forgotten how to cook but she bought enormous stacks of things. The refrigerator was stuffed and the cupboards were full of cans and little packages. Everything else was, in fact, stocked with everything advertised on TV since 1967. The bathroom cabinets were full of bottles for every imaginary ailment. Mother had what she called "palpitations," a series of flutters which she described with movements of her fingertips like wings. When these flutters at-

12

tained the mad pace of horror there was a sudden "heart attack." She had found no doctor who would agree with her. Her disease was too subtle.

Mother looked at Alice, his wife, the way a person at a party throws furtive glances at the mirror. What she saw must have pleased her, the ribbons weren't out of place, because she smiled at her. At Lucian, his son, she looked in amazement. She was a grandmother. Was it an indictment or a blessing? How could that be? How could anything be? It was. It amazed him to see what kind of realities or illusions hovered between this mother and son. A person without a mother must be amazing. The millions of things *in loco parentis*.

She had never liked the way things were. In her conversation as well as in her dreams there was always a place in the past when things had been better. Sometimes there was a place in the future. Rarely. The present was always tyrannical, faceless, fraught with dangers. Well, it was. For her it was. Here, in Washington, D.C., she lived in a hostile jungle of murderers and cold people. A man had been killed in her parking lot. Another had been killed on the corner. Her neighbors did not talk to anybody. They traded words through the crack in the door held by an inside latch. On TV, the news commentators traded murder stories like chewing gum wrappers and, in her own head, visions of doom and despair overtook and chased each other like autumn clouds. She had always had nightmares. It was her common privilege to dwell, at night, in the midst of burning houses, earthquakes, floods and pogroms. In Washington, D.C., her nightmares seeped into the day and everything became the murky grey of fear.

She had been used to another life. People in the old country may not have been always kind, but, at least, they talked to each other, they were interested in each other. She had never seen the likes of America where people don't say hello on the street, don't even acknowledge each other with their eyes. People here had fear in their hearts, and Mother, who had always had fear in hers, did not like to see herself mirrored in a million directions in the country she had chosen to free her of fear. She had not even seen this much fear in Rumania in the worst days after the war.

13

He remembered how much he used to love her. Whenever her men left her, Mother would go into unending fits of despair and threatened to wash the world away with her tears. He had been so terrified of her despair, so afraid that he would lose her. He used to think that if she died, he would too by killing himself. He even fantasized how he would do it. With a knife. A kitchen knife. And then what happened? Her son, her beloved son, did not fit into the mold of what the world should be. She didn't know for sure how the world should be, but she imagined it polite, well dressed, rich, powerful and well fed.

–I had a letter, she said, from your Aunt Elena. She says that your old wife told everybody in the country that you were shot in the leg at a peace demonstration. That poor girl. . . .

She was feeling very sorry for Kira whom she had, since, forgiven for marrying her son at such a tender age.

–How is Kira? he asked.

–Oh, you know, the poor girl had her reputation ruined when you left. . . .

–I heard that she's doing very well, actually. Her stories are being published in books and she has remarried.

–That may be, said Mother, but I know she's not happy. Very flattering. But so untrue.

–And then I had a job teaching poetry in schools. I taught in special schools, in prisons, in kindergartens.

–That was a very good job, said Alice, it was only once a week and he only had to teach for ten weeks.

–Bah! said Mother. I worked for twenty-five years. I worked ever since I was a little girl. I was fourteen when I started working as an apprentice to a photographer and I never stopped. I have to work a lot more here because they don't recognize my years in Rumania . . . The union, you know. . . .

–And then I started writing my autobiography. . . .

–Your autobiography? exploded Mother. You're barely old enough to wipe your nose. What do you have to write about? *I* should write my autobiography. I lived. I had a hard life.

14

Undoubtedly, it was true. She should write her autobiography. But mother wasn't about to sit down and write. She was joking.

The next day they went shopping. The shopping complex they went to was one of those self-contained worlds that thrive on their arrogant assumptions of every need. He hated to shop with Mother. He always had. As a child, she took him to shops and always chose everything for him. She dressed him up according to a picture in her head.
—What clothes you used to have . . . she reminisced. You were the best dressed child on the whole block . . . You had on handknit pants and silk shirts and a little Tyrolese hat with a feather in it . . . Everybody used to look at us when we walked down the street.

When they got home burdened by bundles full of extraordinary compromise, mother sighed: "You never want beautiful things. You like to wear rags." Lucian, surrounded by a sturdy green alligator, the bright red cars of an electric train and the awesome roundness of a yellow beach ball, ran around the apartment.

All in the Family was on TV. Mother loved to see the cast shouting, stomping feet, laughing and screaming, although she understood not a word of what was being said. They looked like real people to her. Mother herself, when she spoke, lifted her eyebrows, shook her head, spread her fingers, lifted her arms, wiggled her foot, laughed in multilevel ways, enclosed herself in the wonderfully intact puppet of her day and country.
—I read *Time* magazine, said Mother when All in the Family stopped, and it says in there that sixty or ninety thousand books are published every year and out of those only seven make money.
—The books I write don't make any money. . . .
—Well, don't forget to put your Aunt Elena in your autobiography. She was nice to us. She took care of you when you were a baby. I don't expect you'll say anything nice about me but, then, that's life . . . I never thought my son would do anything like that . . . She was accusing herself of a mysterious failure. . . .

15

Alone in the bedroom, later (Mother insisted that they take her bed), he stayed awake for a long time telling himself the kind of story he felt he should have told his mother. He was probably dreaming it because he was in a car as he told this story and it had the kind of road feeling to it that all good stories should have.

–Mother, I think you should know that my life is terribly busy . . . Oh, I don't do much but I become fascinated, obsessed and kidnapped by all kinds of things. My past has or is burning up.

No, no, what kind of way is that to speak to one's mother?

The story he would tell would be more like: Dear Mother, The shark-azure sky of the Rivieras is beautiful. Wish you were here to end the day, as we do, with a swim in the buff. No, no. People don't talk like postcards.

Yes, Mother, he would actually say, there is no reason for talking. Why all the talking? Why don't you take me in your arms and let me suckle at your breast and I will be a baby again and then you can put the Tyrolese hat on me. Why did it ever occur to me to leave you? I was paying you back perhaps for sending me to the barber. But the real reason is that I couldn't help it. It isn't me that isn't a baby any more, it's someone else I picked up quite accidentally, a person that's been with me for a long time and who lives in my heart and brain and I can't get him out. It writes poetry. It walks on strange streets. It's half-drunk, half-sober. It loves what it sees. It is irresponsible. It is dark. It is very late. As for me, the baby, I have no say over it because I can't talk. My tongue has been cut.

No, no, any story he would tell his mother would be mostly a story to which no reply was possible. And where was one to find that kind of story? Mother was that kind of story. The Father, the Son and the Holy Ghost were another story but, taken together, they might have been a no-contest story, who knows. A story to which no reply was possible was not, certainly, an autobiography. And yet, what could anyone reply to *his* life? Would a thousand witnesses rise from their metaphorical graves to throw their versions against his? Of course not. The only person in the world that he conceded the right to come forward and say: "I was there and nothing of the sort happened," was his father, but his father, see, had *not* been there and, very likely, he would never be back.

16

BOOK ONE

1

There is a Jewish mythological character who takes on the personality of whomever he happens to be standing next to. This proves so annoying, in the Hasidic tale, that he is put in jail. There, he immediately becomes the jailer. Nothing can be done. Now imagine another mythical character, this one only half-Jewish, who becomes exactly *the opposite* of whomever he is sitting next to. In romantic and existentialist literature this type of hero is given great credit because of his conscious effort to stay this way. In reality, there is no effort. This process of perpetual revolt is involuntary. On the contrary, his deepest wish is to be like everybody else. But due to an organic imbalance, this is impossible.

The person referred to here was floating in amniotic fluid inside his mother's womb one fine afternoon in August 1946, while at the lavishly set dinner table, his mother and his grandfather were involved in a horrible argument. The old man kept pushing diamonds and jewels at the young woman across the table, between the matzoh soup and the fresh bagels, while she pushed them back with a determined pout. The old man was trying to buy the young woman's consent for marrying his son, the father of the thing inside her. In the Jewish manner, Grandpa was lamenting:
    –Oy Oy. Why is my son so blind? Such stubborn woman!
    And then (because his mother wished more than anything to stay healthy) when the baby kicked her as hard as he could, she lost her composure, and the argument ended. She consented to marry the old man's son.

The photo shop on the main street in town was a present from the old man. The young couple moved into the back of it and began outfitting it with gadgets and new paper decorations. The Nazis started to flee, the times were horrifying and absurd, and the prospects for the shop were dim.

It was always a mystery to be looked into, this survival by the Jews in fascist Rumania, and an even greater mystery how these particular Jews managed to do all the crazy things they did under the shadow of the gestapo. An enormous statue fell on the father's foot once during a forced work program, but he got up intact. Which was very lucky because the statue was full of explosives carved into it by partisans. The unexploded representation of General Bratu on his horse was gingerly lifted by the rest of the work crew, some of whom were in the know, some of whom had no idea, and restored to its equestrian erectness in front of the German Kommandantur in Piazza Victoria. As Father limped away as fast as he could, the explosion turned the square to shambles. In this way did fate intervene, a method of intervention which the unborn baby was to inherit.

Grandfather paternal had a bazaar where he sold cheap trinkets, while in the back they had resistance meetings and poker games, Russian roulette and clandestine Jewish services. Protected as they were by some wayward angel, when the gestapo began poking around, the old man's crazy manner misled them into thinking the noise came from across the street and they soon arrested a completely Aryan gendarme's family residing there. Sixteen years later, in the lobby of a movie house, the young progeny of these people was accosted by an ugly old crone who began to scream in a crazy-prophetic manner:

–Your grandfather was a thief. He stole our gold. He gave it back to no one, may he rot in hell where the purple crows feed on Jew meat. And your father was a whore. Every woman in town came under his power. I personally kept the room he rented from me for two lousy cents a day where he brought his tramps, malignant queers, bestial phonies.

20

Everyone was listening. Was it true? Perhaps. It is very possible that, beside being partisans, they had been pirates. And, as for his father's women, he knew all about them. They later became his mother's favorite recollection. He rather admired him for it.

So, while his father and his grandfather practiced resistance, piracy and sex, his pregnant mother was taking photographs of fleeing Nazis who posed sadly with their local German girlfriends. Suddenly, the Nazis fled to the accompaniment of sad sentimental harmonicas while the population of the town (which was mostly Sass, Transylvanian Germans) threw flowers and candies after them.

The Russians were coming.

Standing up in her 1933 dress with a flapper hat on her pretty red curls and a glass of champagne in her hand, the soon-to-be mother followed the armored divisions crawling grimly West and had, in a flash, the brilliant idea of giving her baby a Russian name so that when the bloodthirsty Bolsheviks stomped through the neat little flower garden, they would be stopped dead in their tracks by this act of etymological devotion.

Andrei Ivanovitch began to squirm.

As the German tanks receded behind clouds of dust, father came home, and when he heard his baby's new name, he began laughing. He finally controlled himself and, drawing his breath, he told the mother that:

–*One* The Russians were our friends.
–*Two* That he was the commander of the famed *Rumanian Trees*, the partisan regiment which was famous the world over.
–*Three* That when the Russians came they would kiss embrace toast and decorate us.

This, mother could not believe, but later that evening, when the song "Katiusha" began echoing from the distance, her husband passed by the window of the photo shop dressed in military fatigues waving a machine gun and followed closely by fifty famil-

21

iar looking men, all her neighbors, shouting: SPASIBA! SPASIBA! SPASIBA! Everyone else stood behind locked doors or else were burying German paraphernalia under the floors.

Well, the Russians filled the streets and their wild parties began. They seemed completely oblivious to the town population, and soon a bunch of courageous young girls appeared on the street. They came out partly because of the adventure and the good-looking soldiers and partly prodded by the folks inside who were beginning to die of hunger.

Just as his father had said, his family was soon invited to dinner by General Azamov, and the Third Order of Stalin was pinned to his chest among champagne toasts and clouds of smoke.

The soldiers were rather shy and gentlemanly and a lot more interested in the young lady's charms than in the name of the strangely named brat howling in her womb. And they loved to be photographed.

The shop's inventory at the time consisted of two ancient cameras, an enlarger, and a number of cardboard figures of generals on horses and tuxedoed dandies holding beautiful cardboard girls by thin 1920s waists. These figures had holes cut in them where the heads should have been and the customers stuck their own heads in the holes to be photographed. The Russians went wild over these, sticking their blond, black and brown heads in and out of these figures all day long.

The young lady, who did not look very pregnant, was adjusting a head in a hole overlooking a cardboard lake, a flaky boat, a stiff girl and a flaky moon when sudden sharp pains swept her off her feet.

Even at the hospital, he was undecided on the issue of whether or not he should get born. Moving his eyes slowly over the hanging intestines and undigested hunks of beans and fat which had been his home, he decided to see the rest of the world. In the

22

room next to them a stillborn child had been delivered. This information, communicated subtly to him, made up his mind. He would not be dead. As long as he would live, he would not be dead! He screamed and, voilà, This World!

In the cab back from the hospital, he struck no sound and the cabdriver turned away from his horses, which were proceeding leisurely up the cobbled street, and told his mother:
   –He's a snail-baby, that little devil!
   –Snail?
   –Salty and folded in, that is, ma'm. In our part of the country we call them snail-babies 'cause they don't talk till they are four years old.
   –What kind do you have? said mother.
   –Mine are screamers, ma'm, frog-babies! Their insides is lined with hot peppers, hot sausages and eighty proof *tzuica*. Har Har Har.

But the cabdriver was wrong. The reason he had stopped squealing was his secret suspicion that his mother had no brain of her own and that, while he was in her womb, he had supplied her with all her ideas. A second after his birth, a puzzled expression had come upon her face and, from that moment, it never left her.

During her days in the hospital, most uniformed Russians had gone on West, leaving behind all the shadowy civilian ones. His father and his group had followed them West.

The country settled comfortably back into its long and ancient history of riots, assassination, turmoil and gossip. The photo shop, under strange management, acquired a number of more modern-looking cardboard figures while the baby howled unattended in the darkroom, propped between a tray of developing fluid and an enormous pile of unclaimed pictures.

The king resigned, leaving his country, a fugitive, and headed straight for his Swiss bank accounts. The Communists came to power. His father returned but disappeared immediately on a

23

strange mission. The dictator of the country was a woman. The world's first woman dictator, Ana Pauker, had a short haircut and a dry voice. Under her direction, thousands of political "enemies" were eliminated, including thousands of peasants who refused to go along with collectivization.

Everyone, however, loved photographs and the photo shop was humming. The cardboard figures were going out of style. The baby howled insults to the customers. His mother began several romances.

One day, a big red shawl was brought in. Mama wrapped Baby in it and got on a bus. Two days later, after miles of fields, rivers and ruins they arrived at the ancient city of Alba Iulia, which means White Dawn Julia. The little red bundle was delivered to a tall gaunt woman with a sharp nose.
    —Kiss your grandmother! said Mama.
    Baby wet his diaper.

2

Alba Iulia, this provincial capital from the heyday of the Austro-Hungarian Empire, when there used to be splendid carriages and elegant shoppers eating ice creams under parasols, was a bleak hot hole that day. There were no people on the streets, the huge castles and fortifications were mute on the hills, the flies were asleep. Baroness Kodaly, his grandmother, had been reduced from her baronial splendor to the misery of raising and selling chickens in the marketplace. She was still, however, living in her ancient castle at the end of Murez Hill. This castle, built by Janosz Kodaly some six hundred years previous, was a drafty stone immensity. His grandmother used only two rooms on the ground floor, the former servants kitchens next to the big old kitchen. The rest of the monstrosity was inhabited by spiders, bats, ghosts and various astral species. His grandmother dropped him on an elephant-sized pillow and said to his mother (who was buttoning her coat to catch the next bus back to Sibiu):

–Are you still married to that photographer?

–No.

–There is still God!

–I left two bottles, ten new red diapers and a music box behind him.

–Your father said you were a boy.

–I have to leave now, mother. Kiss Aunt Elena for me.

His mother was gone for four years.

The chickens lived all over the right wing of the castle, in the bathrooms and alongside the bed, laying random eggs everywhere

25

and, it seems, under the infant's rubber sheet which got very wet when he moved. His grandmother (who was also blind) spanked him for wetting his bed until she took the sheet out for airing and got yolk all over herself. Then she spanked him again out of shame for having spanked him in the first place. He didn't know why, but these second spankings made him feel a lot better.

He spent most of his day in the marketplace, snuggled between tied-up chickens hanging upside down from long bamboo poles.

This is why his first sounds were not human. They were in chickenese, chicken language.
Crrroaaarrk! Cooorrkkkak! Crrwerrk! Crrrrrroarrktk! Ktttttrrrrraskrrrk! Kaarrrrorrrrtttttk! Crrrrorlkkkkr! Caaaorrrk!

This brought on a series of fresh spankings to which he got very wise very fast, and without abandoning his knowledge of the chicken language, he began making startlingly human sounds. These sounds were not really human but his grandmother didn't notice. These were sounds composed by simplifying and slowing down chicken words.

His toilet training must have been exceedingly difficult in the Kodaly castle because the Baroness herself used an oversized marble bidet with angel handles which she emptied out the window and he does not remember any other container for excrement. Oh no, wait! He now remembers, or thinks he does, a Chinese soup bowl with gold dragons on it into which he . . . Oh, God! Into which he bends and drinks the thick brown water. What's this all about? He will return to this matter later in this narrative.

There were smells, of course. The decaying stone castle smelled like a thousand years of suppressed shivers. The sweat of condensation, the sweets of condescension. Apples, pears, preserves, wines in lost cellars in unknown areas of the castle which his grandmother didn't remember . . . Old leather harnesses . . . Tons of trunks, pictures, old metal . . . Special zero-degree creatures stuck between air molecules . . . Leaves in the fall . . . Smells of

26

hundred-year-old feasts shooting down shafts into his room
. . . smells of political conversations . . . Cheese, smoke and fires
. . . And floating under and over everything like a thin, melodious
veil, the smell of chickenshit, the eternal, marvelous smell of
chickenshit.

Grandmother's favorite pose was sitting on a decayed divan with
her eyes on the ceiling, one hand over her heart and the other
hand moving constantly up and down her body looking for lumps.
These lumps, she said, come from nowhere without a sound and
suddenly you have to have them cut out. He looked at her for
hours imagining small bands of lumps hovering around the window waiting to pounce on Granma. Sometimes he would go
further and imagine the lumps entering Granma and roving inside her body at fantastic speeds, much faster than her hand
which always touched the spot where a lump had just been.

The Baroness spoke German, and it is in this language that he first
heard the story of his grandfather.

The Baron had just exited the main gate of the Officers Academy
with his new captain's tresses on his young shoulders, when
Granma walked by. Struck by her blinding beauty he immediately
began showing his medals to her. This was so much against the
Code that Grandmother ran home crying and didn't stop for a
week. Her father, Baron Geza, seeing his daughter's unhappiness,
pulled on his white gloves which were made of the finest silk, and
sought out the young captain. It is not very clear what went on
between the two gentlemen, but soon they both appeared at the
Geza castle on horseback wearing their best clothes. The young
captain fell on his knees and implored her to marry him. She put
him off for a year and then called on him. He was still waiting
and crying. This broke her heart and she married him. There
followed thirty years of marriage about which we know nothing.
Then, one day, as he was coming home from a routine inspection
of his gold mines, two bandits overtook his carriage and split his
head open with an iron ax. This was ironic because everything on
the Baron was gold. His watch, his rings, his teeth and his shirt.

27

When Grandmother was told of his death, she lost her eyesight. She threw all the servants out of the house except six of them and saw nobody. Finally, just ten years previous, she opened some of the letters on the huge unopened pile in the antechamber and had Aunt Elena read her the contents. She was informed in these that she had lost the mines and had no more money, none at all. After selling what she could, but not the relics and certainly not the castle, she was slowly steered by Aunt Elena in the direction of chicken-raising.

The baby would listen to these tales, looking at the clouds. The clouds looked like his grandfather, the two bandits, the letters, the towers, the gold mines. But he would not say any words. He had even stopped using the slightly human sounds he had previously used to fool the Baroness.

For four more years he would not talk.

—It is people's secrets that are more interesting, said his grandmother. What they say does not matter. But it takes a lot of talking to get people to listen to your silences. She would sigh. Better never to talk.

It felt good to know that his grandmother knew that he could talk but would not. This mutual confidence made one the ideal listener, the other the ideal talker. And whatever silent wisdom had been absorbed from that woman was at the root of all later wisdom.

She was a great storyteller. With the exception of her life, which she romanticized, all her stories were filled with a touch of common sense. She told fairy tales in an ironical manner, adding thousands of hilarious details to, let's say, Cinderella's life. Where else could one find out that Cinderella had "a thing for soldiers" and that she wasn't a very good housekeeper because there was always dust in the corners and under the beds? Or that Snow White was really pretty black inside because mirrors lie and because sin is really like a roving lump: no one sees it but it's always ahead of you.

28

Rare people visited the house. There was Aunt Elena who, it was whispered, married someone of no rank. This someone was completely invisible, but Aunt Elena's imposing figure (as skinny but taller than Grandmother's) could be seen from a large distance because she swayed and coughed as she walked. She always had a basket of homemade goodies about her and she would bend down to Baby and stick a sweet finger filled with cake icing into his throat. Sometimes she would take him for walks through melancholy old deserted mansions, down past the burnt down Geza castle, all the way to the *Center*, as they called the Main Street. In the Center there was a park, pushcarts with ice cream and cotton candy, outdoor coffeehouses, the old Imperial Hotel (now headquarters of the Communist Party), the ruined Roman Bath and numerous hat shops, barbershops and bakeries.

–Bah, she would say, your mother was no good. She toasted the Germans when she was sixteen, and then married a Jew . . . Either one or the other . . . If you do both it's like being either a man or a woman. If a woman could pass for a German, she could surely pass for a man . . . And vice versa.

All her speeches had this kind of logic in them. Logic was, alas, his weakest point, so he would listen fascinated. She would meet someone on the street:
–Good to see you, Maria (this with a baronial sneer and gaze). You look good . . . Your heart must be rotten. . . .
–Doing all we can, Baroness, all we can.
–Tell me something: is there still a flour rationing program?
–No, no, Baroness, they changed that six months ago. Don't you eat bread?
–*I* certainly don't.
Her interlocutor would give the child a worried look, shaking her head as if to say "the crazy old lady," and then she'd say:
–Children need bread!
–Him (she would point her lorgnette at him), he eats potatoes and chicken.
This was true. His entire diet until the age of four consisted of apples, chicken and potatoes. The chicken was boiled, fried, or in

29

soup form. They ate no eggs because the Baroness abhorred "the stuff inside." The potatoes were always boiled. Salt was a rare commodity. He never acquired a taste for it. Chicken liver (fried) was a delicacy and he had chicken livers every Sunday.

He had no friends but he would endlessly explore the castle getting lost and meeting ghosts. Among old weapons, old trunks and abandoned towers he was surrounded by a ghost population which gave him gifts and followed him everywhere, listening to his every whim. This phantom army was at his disposal twenty-four hours a day. He gave orders, sent them on absurd missions, commanded their positions. And the phantoms, happy to play because they had all eternity, obeyed him faithfully.

Many years later, he wondered about the accessibility of his phantom army. Back then, all he had to do was call on them with the three secret words (. . . . .) and they would turn the world upside down. Now, the decision to ask for their help has become more and more difficult. The phantoms, because they have all eternity, are still playing. But he . . . he does not know. No, not for sure.

It was the month of January 1950. There was snow on the ground. Thick snow. The mountains were completely covered. An elegant lady rang the bell. She had come to take him back.
    –He still doesn't speak, said Grandmother.
    –I don't care! I just want him, I need him, I can't live without him!
    –Are you married?
    –No, Mother.
    –Better this way. Your father always said you were a boy.
    –Kiss Aunt Elena for me, will you?

They caught the next bus back to Sibiu.

3

Mama is back! O great bus! Mimicry! Ascension! Power! Somnambulism! Whenever the bus ground to a halt, the peasants shoved in. At every stop they took the bus by storm carrying wheels of cheese, caged chickens, bloody carcasses, tied bundles and sticks. Their bark shoes sank into the metal floor. Perched on her knees, on his mama's knees, he adored her perfume, he snuggled up to her breasts, he was very small again. When the bus rolled out of a small village, the peasants fell asleep only to wake up with a great gasp at the next stop where a new wave of peasants squeezed violently in. His mama's perfume mixed with the sweat, and with the mountains, fields and rivers rolling by out the window. They were lucky to have a seat. They were lucky in everything. They were immortal. The sweat-soaked objects of trade in the bus and their owners began to cook subtly in the heat. Did someone faint? His mother caressed his head. Mama hugged him close. Her mouth was at crotch level with the enormous dismembered peasant leaning over a dead pig. Her lips were pointed down in disgust. Her nose was wrinkled, but her eyes, half-closed, enveloped her son with warmth. Were the birds of old romance leaving her head at that moment? He did not remember his mother very well. But he felt good on her knees. A great chicken cry of gratitude echoed through him. They were home.

—It is a big room, Mother said, as big as one can find these days.

It was. There was a copper bed with tall posts on which someone had carved Greek gods at play and work. A bedside table with a round mirror. A small window. A closet without a door filled

31

with dresses imbued with Mother's perfume. A lithograph of horses grazing in a green substance.

They shared the kitchen. He was to find out who they shared it with a few moments later when he decided he was hungry and started running down the narrow hallway to where he thought the kitchen might be. He opened a yellow door and saw a naked little girl with her foot raised in the air. The next moment she lunged at him and hit him with her foot under his knee. He reeled. He fell. Began to howl. How could a naked foot hurt so much?
  –Excuse us, said Mother, pulling him off the floor, the little boy thought this was the kitchen.

He took a look into the room as he was being dragged out and saw the first Hieronymus Bosch picture in his life: a gaunt man in striped yellow pajamas sat on a bed with death on his face. Kneeling at his feet, an old hag in rags held a shaving brush full of white cream to his cavernous face, while her other hand brandished an enormous old-fashioned razor. The room was (otherwise) empty. Steam was rising from the floor and the little girl, who had just kicked him, stood laughing with her hands on her entirely white hips, stretching her entirely naked body, with the exception of the wooden clogs on her feet, which, for the first time, he noticed. The door closed with a bang behind them.
  –That was simply dreadful of that little girl. But we have to live together . . . so tomorrow you be nice to her, hear . . . ?
  –I'm not that hungry, he said.

These were his first words. They had escaped from within him like a coiled spring. They came out of his mouth like a flawless bowel movement. It was his first breakdown. Goodbye, great nothing!

Mother, surprised, jerks her head from him to the ceiling in total awe. Her eyes fill with tears.
  –You said something you did my sweet baby you did you said it You're not very hungry you say! You're not? What do you want to eat? What do you want me to buy you to eat? You can have anything you want to eat. . . .

He didn't know that there were other things to eat. Chicken and potatoes were all he knew. But he was glad. Mother danced with him all around the room. She had been so afraid, she said, that her little baby would be mute and, you know, in this world, you just *have* to talk. How else could you get yourself a girl?

To please her, he began to talk. He would not stop. He put together all the words he ever heard, at random, with pauses only for shallow breaths, thousands of beautiful endless words, a kaleidoscope of three, four languages, German, Hungarian, Rumanian and Chickenese. Words, words, rains of them falling over all the planet with equal abandon, covering the world with a layer of water or snow. This layer would get thicker with the years, would cover everything, the landscape would be unrecognizable. And then they would bury him in it, in all the sounds he would ever make, they would bury him in this vortex of music where he would live for thousands of years, vibrating without relief.

—In the daytime, until about five, I will be in the photo shop working to keep us in bonbons, said Mama, patting his cheek. Then I will come home. Ilse will take care of you until I return.

A night full with words passed.
—There is Ilse now, said Mother.
A tower of meat topped by a black bonnet faced him from the heights. Two powerful breasts squeezed in by iron brassieres thrust into the air above his head.
—This is Andrei Ivanovitch, Fräulein.

All the words that had made him invincible the previous night vanished when Ilse's round, sea-monster eyes took him in, while her lips, two tiny purple lines, tightened and disappeared into each other.

Ilse made chicken soup. He sat in a corner touching his forehead to his foot one thousand times and one thousand more. He could hear their neighbors, whom he had seen the day before, frying

33

bacon on the burner. The little girl walked past him. Does she see him? When his foot touches his head for the zillionth time, he feels a surge of power. He looks up. The little girl is grinning. He boldly lets his eyes take her in and then he slips inside her. He is in her mind. He knows what it is to be that little girl. He looks at Ilse. She frowns. He slips inside her. Brrrr. Why is it so cold in there? What is she so angry about? He comes out. The little girl leaves the kitchen.

The chicken soup is ready. Ilse pours some in a big bowl. This is not like Grandmother's. There are onions in it. Little fried onions. And pieces of dough. He eats some. Then he stops.

–Eat, hisses Ilse.
The neighbors turn from their stoves. Although they can't understand German, they relish the scene.
–No, he says.
Ilse lowers her eyes until they touch his face.
–I don't like you, Jewboy! If you don't eat you have to be punished.

He pushes the bowl in her face. The hot soup shoots up in a yellow jet and scalds the underwater eyes, the thin lips, the small tongue sticking out of her mouth. She shrieks. Suddenly, he is way up in the air, suspended by the ears from her knobby fingers.
There was a little boy in the Black Forest, she says to the airborne creature twisting in her hands, who disobeyed his Fräulein. He was cooked and eaten. Yes, yes, cooked and eaten. Cooked and eaten.

This makes a great impression. Cooking, of all things, makes him sick. How would he taste? Then, by some mysterious process, he goes, again, inside the little girl who has reappeared in the doorway. She feels sorry for him. He twists and shrieks.
The other two are laughing.

When he is finally released, he collapses in his old corner. Everything hurts. His neighbors return to their bacon. A whole list of

34

numbers appears in his head. They are the endless dates that his Grandmother used to recite to him. They are the dates of births, anniversaries, weddings and deaths of everyone Grandmother had ever known. The memory of the Baroness is filled with these numbers. He knows what they look like because he knows all the numbers from one to ten from a book Aunt Elena brought him. He wants to be with Aunt Elena. The numbers move before his eyes. What is it? Yes, yes, these numbers are magical. You can make people do things with numbers. He remembers birthdays. How everyone runs around. The excitement. Aunt Elena.

–10–20–1856 10–12–1879, he whispers, invoking Aunt Elena by her birth and marriage dates.
She appears.
They talk.
–You look rotten. Your heart must be overflowing.
–It's because of Ilse. She pulls my ears.
–This Ilse will burn in hell but until then . . . let's see . . . Can you do this?

The Baroness leans on her carved cane and shows him a secret hand signal, thumb down—index up—thumb up—index down—three times.

He tries it. There is a slight effect on Ilse but it's hard to tell.

That night, when Mama came home, he did not talk to her. He didn't ever want to talk to her, to anyone, for that matter. Later on, he is stretched out next to her in the big copper bed, but he can't sleep. Why did Mama leave him with Ilse after coming back for him? Maybe she is not his Mama at all, maybe she wants to cook and eat him. He dozes off but wakes up immediately because his mother has become a putrid mass of flesh radiating cold and little blue lights. His hand gropes for her! It's true! Lying next to him is the icy corpse of a horrible witch! Never in his wanderings through the Kodaly castle had he seen such a creature! It is terrible! A green slime oozes down the sheet up into the crease next to him. He makes himself very small. He calls his phantom army. They don't come. He is now smaller than a bug. He rolls over and gets very far away, at an immense distance from the body next to him. At this distance he can sleep. And so it came to pass that, from then on, our hero could not sleep next to anyone without first rolling very far away, at a distance of at least a thousand miles, where they cannot touch him while he's asleep.

Next day, Mother's new beau, the captain, was introduced. The captain was very stiff, smelled like eau de cologne, and barked when he laughed.
    —You will sleep at Ilse's tonight, Mother said, wrapping herself around the uniformed absurdity sitting on the bed.
    —No, no, dear Aunt Elena, get me out of here. Granma, please!

It was winter, a ferocious winter, the kind of winter that makes the blood freeze and pits the entire landscape against an icy sheet of hard starlight. Merciless mountain winter. Ilse dragged him by the hand through the empty streets, lit here and there by ancient gas lamps.

    —Once upon a time, she was saying, in the Black Forest . . . (she introduced all her speeches with this and thus made everything allegorical. In his later mind, allegory became, par excellence, the medium of violence) . . . there was a little boy like you who couldn't do anything and didn't eat his food. The wolves came and asked him three questions. If he could not answer, they were going to eat him. Do you obey your Fräulein? First question. Do you eat all your food? Second question. Are you a Jewboy? Third question. So the wolves ate him because the boy said nothing.

In the little shack where Ilse lived, the Black Forest grew right through the walls. There was only a small bed, a big stone to sit on and a little woodstove. She made a fire. He stood up looking at her in a kind of terrified torpor. She was going to burn him to death in the little stove. An old woman bent over hot bricks. As earlier, his mind searched for magic. There were no numbers in his head and he did not remember the words which summoned his secret armies. The shadows of the flames were on the walls.

36

For the third time that day, Ilse pulls his ears. Then she orders him to take off all his clothes and get into bed. It is freezing cold. He jumps into bed and pulls the covers over his head. He shuts his eyes and makes himself small to roll away. But he is caught by Ilse who is bringing hot bricks into the bed with a huge pair of tongs. She drops them at his feet, sighs, and, with one hand, unfastens the enormous dress floating around her like a cupola. Ilse is an onion. Under that dress there is another one. And another one. She becomes smaller and smaller, only her breasts do not grow any smaller. She must be a young woman! Up until this time, he had seen an old hag. It makes no difference. Pulling a long grey flannel shirt over her head, Ilse jumps into bed. She takes him in her arms. He is shivering. "Put your feet on the bricks, boy." This is it. He slides down, grinding his teeth, and puts his feet on the bricks. They feel nice. His hand reaches out and he grabs Ilse by a thick forest of hair between her legs. "Hee, hee, hee," laughs the woman. He falls asleep. But not before rolling away into his distance.

Mother's captain was becoming permanent and although Andrei now knew Ilse's secret soft spot, and could stop her from killing him, he wanted to get away. The captain had an acquaintance in Hochstadt, the old part of town, who, he said, would be happy to take care of the kid for a fee.

The gendarme and his wife were not bad people. They were fond of children. Their son was a railroad engineer who had become "a great chief" in the Railroad Ministry. His picture hung over the bed in which they all slept, and the lines in the doorway marked his growth from age one. Andrei Ivanovitch was immediately put against this doorway and it was discovered, this way, that at the age of four and a half he was just as tall as the engineer had been.

Although apparently Christian, these folks belonged to a very old anthropomorphic order which worshipped the sun and cherished Dacian gods. What the worship consisted of was made very clear to him one day when, after lying for hours in the sun outside, he

37

got a little dizzy and came back inside saying,
—Goddam the sun!
He received a prompt blow across the face.—Don't ever say
that, whispered Veta, and he knew that he wouldn't.
He felt so guilty, in fact, that for the rest of his life, every
morning or afternoon, whenever the sun came out or left, he
whispered under his breath: Excuse me, sun! I didn't mean it!

Besides initiating him into pagan practices, the gendarme and his
wife let him have free rein of the street and he entered, for the
first time, Sibiu's street life. The streets were narrow and twisting
and became lost under walls or inside houses or continued on to
turn into paths leading straight up the Carpathian Mountains
which embraced the town from all sides with their white peaks.
It was easy to get lost. The two main gangs in the neighborhood
weren't much interested in the small boy watching them, so he
could follow their activities relatively unobserved. He followed
the bigger boys as far as they would let him go, and, occasionally,
when they had forgotten him, he would lose them and the awesome strangeness of the place and the fact that he was five years
old would overcome him and he would turn into a little scared
animal clawing his way home on scent alone. But he always got
there. Sibiu was a big town. It had a hundred thousand inhabitants and millions of wandering ghosts. It had five movie theaters,
opera, and the most interesting sewer tops in the world. It had
the oldest gas lamps in Europe and the first tramways in Rumania.
It had been a bourgeois Mecca since the beginning of the Middle
Ages. It was German, Lutheran, Magyar, Catholic, Rumanian,
Orthodox. It was a mysterious and, occasionally, a prosperous
town. But it wasn't prosperous then. In fact, it was downright
poor. Gypsies, the other inhabitants of the street, roamed around
in great numbers, read palms and coffee, got into fights, pitched
pennies, poisoned dogs and constantly touched their privates.
They were, to be sure, on constant lookout for something to steal
but since there weren't many stealable things around they had
little luck. People were, in fact, so poor that any such luxury as
an extra pair of shoes was guarded better than the crown jewels
by sleeping with them.

When the gendarme and his wife were asleep in the afternoon (they took regular naps), he passed the time playing with the old clocks in the drawer of the old dresser. He took them apart and then put the pieces back in the drawer until, after many afternoons, they filled it. There were marvelous wheels, springs, screws, numbers and hands. It occurred to him that if he put them back together he could take them apart again, so he started putting them back at random, fitting things wherever they fit. Soon he had built a large mechanical lump with strings sticking out of it. It was beautiful. Not only did he not want to ever take it apart again, but he was immensely proud of it. Who should he show it to? The policeman was gruffy when woken up. He thought of the girl next door.

He slipped the thing in his pocket, climbed the fence that separated them, walked through a window and, poof, he was in her living room. She looked as if she had been waiting for him.

Without a word, he pulled the thing from his pocket and showed it to her. She examined it carefully, took it away from him, put it to her little ear and then drummed on it a few times with her knuckles. Then they took each other's hand and went under the piano.
    –I will show you mine if you show me yours, she said. See? She lifted her little skirt.

He saw the tiny opening in her hairless, beautiful mound and his breath stopped. As if dreaming, he pulled his out of his spielhosen. It was hard. Her hand touched it. A wave of warmth and happiness rushed through them. She kept her hand there.

Suddenly, there was the girl's mother.
    –Don't you ever come around here, bad boy!!
    She threw his watch animal after him as he went out the window. It landed on the cement and fell apart.

His mind was seething with revenge. He was hurt, bitter. The girl next door merges with him, while his mother, Ilse, and the girl's

39

mother merge with each other. Then Grandmother and Aunt Elena merge with him and the girl too and now they stand, facing each other, these two feminine conglomerates, glaring, sizzling at each other. He leads his corporation to victory. His mother, Ilse and the other, burn. But soon he is very sorry. He does not want his mother to burn. Only Ilse. Not even Ilse. "Excuse me, sun! I didn't mean it!"

It was not long after this that he opened his first picture book. It was full of pirates. Mother, who was an infrequent visitor at the gendarme's house, watched him motion mysteriously at burning ships somewhere behind her shoulders, and said:
　—He's a dead likeness of his father!

Where was his father?

4

He was getting a little confused from speaking German with his mother *(Gottseidank, Schatzichen)*, Hungarian to his grandmother *(Egyi io Istenem)*, Rumanian to the retired policeman *(Du-te-n māta, Domnule)*, Russian to his friends *(Za mir schto Boje)* and some kind of chicken language to himself *(Dabooddadbacrrroaarcboom)*.

But this confusion soon was relieved by the big wooden gun that the policeman made him. Armed to the teeth, he now patrolled the streets of his medieval city, rescuing the girl next door from bandits, pirates, fires and floods. This gun gave him a great sense of security and a love for guns that never left him. In his first well-remembered dream, a truck full of soldiers crosses the street in front of old Vlad's Spice Store (a witch's cupboard filled with superstitious herbs) and the soldiers begin to shoot at him. He is hit, falls, but alas, he is only wounded. He picks up his gun and blasts the receding truck. Soldiers blow up in slow motion.

At the height of his gun-toting period he is involved in thousands of rescue missions. One day, coming home terribly tired from a fight with a whole regiment of Napoleonic cavalry, he sees a fantastic car parked in front of the house. He rushes in.

A tall, balding man with a mustache is sitting at the kitchen table. The man picks him up, kisses him and says in Rumanian:

–You recognize me, Don't you? He doesn't but he knows who he is. It is his father.

41

They go for a ride in the car, an event which brings every adult and child within fifty blocks into the street to watch. Cars, you see, are unheard of in this part of town and there are perhaps ten cars in the rest of the town and some fifty BMW motorcycles left over by the Nazis. Gravely resting his gun on the side of the open window, he savors the deliciousness of the moment. Very soon now, when the car will begin to move, he will kill them all. Blam, blam, blam.

They are driving through town. Everywhere they go, people turn around and stare. The town is a very old medieval capital composed of millions of twisting stairways, sudden and sad little plazas shadowed by enormous trees. Gothic cathedrals, secret tunnels, fortifications, monasteries, statues and ogival windows cut like eyes into the slanting roofs.

An aura of prosperity and authority surrounds his father. He is kind. He hands him five leis (read lays) as they are driving. A dollar is worth thirty leis. An engineer makes 260 leis a month. Five leis is a lot. He is invincible now. He has a gun, a car and enough money to pay any fine he would incur jaywalking, driving too fast or whatever.

His father is married, for the fifth time, to a blonde woman who smells like apples; he plays poker all night (not tonight); he drinks huge bottles of *tzuica* (an eighty proof plum brandy) and has a mysterious job in the newly formed but amazingly solid Stalinist government.

Then his father leaves him alone in the car while he goes into a store to buy another bottle. Little Ivanovitch gets behind the wheel, starts the motor and the car begins to move across the street, over the sidewalk, and into the window of the Boodoo Hat Store where it stops in a Chaplinesque scene with thousands of hats collapsing on it. He is unharmed, the car seems okay and the surrounding crowd is laughing. His father makes some ambiguous apologies that sound more like threats and they leave the scene without paying for the window or the hats.

42

Boodoo is one of the last private merchants left in town after the complete confiscation of private enterprise by the government and, as such, he cannot do much against a party official. His father seems pleased, in fact.

–That will show the dirty rat, he says as they drive off, and adds:

–Private enterprise should be open to strange accidents.

Soon, however, Father stops coming for him. He is still waiting, gun in hand, every Saturday, but the familiar motor isn't breaking the peace on the street.

A few months later he hears about it. It seems that his father wasn't a Stalinist in the newly formed Stalinist government and one day some soldiers came, took him and shot him. Public power, he should say, but doesn't know how, should be open to strange accidents.

The random story of his father came slowly in romantic pieces. During the war he had led a small partisan detachment against the Nazis by blowing up trains and shooting German officers. The detachment was really what was left of the Rumanian anarchist movement. When the Communists came to power on the turrets of Russian tanks, his father was awarded the Third Order of Stalin and a highly honorary job in the new government. During the first purge in the new power structure, his father was eliminated.

He was a poet of sorts, this father of his. On the margins of some papers found long after his death, Father had scribbled a poem by Arghezi:

> Never was autumn so good
> to our death-happy soul!

This is a lousy translation, but very little can be translated concerning fathers. They live and die in the original.

Left without a father, holding a gun, he began looking around for a reasonable substitute. Of all the possible candidates, one in particular tickled his imagination and made his heart melt. This

43

was a tall man with a mustache similar to his father's. This man could be seen in pictures all over town, holding little children and smiling a dazzling smile. His name was Stalin. Andrei Ivanovitch was, of course, jealous of Joseph Vissarionovitch Stalin's popularity with so many other children and so he looked for a way to make him his own. This way presented itself quite naturally one day when, passing the window of a bookshop, he saw a little framed portrait of the dictator. He walked in and, with the five leis his father had given him, bought it.

Now there was this picture on the nightstand although there had been a long argument with the retired policeman about putting it on that particular nightstand. He got his way and there it was, smiling under a terrific mustache.

A great secret dialogue ensued between the two. Endearing words were exchanged. Every night he kissed the picture before going to bed, made a complete report on the various glorious armies he had defeated that day, and then concluded with a prayer which his grandmother had taught him but he had never used:

> Our Father who art in Heaven
> Blessed be Thy Name
> Thy kingdom come . . . etc.

Greek Orthodox Style.

Stalin was magnanimous. He stomached it all. Andrei imagined that nobody knew of his secret relations with the great man but, of course, later, he found out that every evening, when the lights were out, children kneeled at their bedsides praying to the same little portrait, since it was mass-produced for that very same reason. Nevertheless, he was a great secret, and he was especially great in the winter when Andrei came home with frozen feet and found the understanding mustache bristling with sympathy from the nightstand.

One day, he was under the kitchen table, playing unseen under somebody's feet. Suddenly, the retired policeman burst in.

–Stalin just died! he said to the somebody in the room.

There was silence. Huge, hot tears invaded him with pain under the table. He had to rush to his little picture. But before he could, the retired policeman added:

–I'm glad the sonofabitch is dead!

His world stopped.

Later on, when everyone was denouncing Stalin, he said nothing. All the bad talk he heard affected him little in the daytime. But at night, it was still the little picture on the nightstand that he would pray to and when there was no more picture it was a picture in his head and when, after years, the picture was erased and an impersonal "it" with a great mustache took its place, he still had words for it.

And when those words, too, went away a great silence came into its place and a great emptiness where something should have been. As for the whole subject of fathers, he suspects a terrible fraud. There are no fathers, he will say, only mustaches which scatter in the wind, hair by hair, which vanish, disappear, betray and leave you alone by night.

5

The old nunnery had been converted into a school some five years previously but the change was not obvious. The gold letters above the main doorway which used to read THE URSULINE MON-ASTERY were faded and had been violently erased, but they still read THE URSULINE MONASTERY. Inside, the square cement yard, shaded by two elms, invoked a great austerity. The classrooms, their angels, icons and gargoyles removed, presented big black holes staring from the ceilings. It was in these holes that his mind was to take repeated trips and come back loaded with curious information. The main meeting hall, without an altar, seemed aimless, so that no matter where one was sitting there was no central focus and, later, when they built a speaker's platform there, the image of impermanence and aimlessness became even stronger. It was in this room that he was made into a pioneer.

–Andrei Ivanovitch Goldmutter, do you swear to always obey the cause of Lenin, Stalin, and the Glorious Communist Party of Rumania?
–I do.

Invisible angels floated out from the tunnels carved underground where the nuns were buried. "Dominus Vobiscum" echoed the immediate past.
He kissed the flag. The taste of silk was overpowering.

He tried the new pioneer salute.

–In the name of Lenin, Stalin and the glorious Communist Party of Rumania, he said with his hand to his temple, Forward!

Pioneers wore red handkerchiefs around their necks. These handkerchiefs were carefully ironed at home by solicitous mothers, and ended up being chewed all the way up to the knot. He began chewing his immediately, a few minutes after being initiated in what was to be the first of a number of organizations into which the youth was neatly packed away by thoughtful elders.

Comrade Pudinca taught reading. Looking at her kind and wrinkled face he felt a warm glow of happiness. This was in spite of her abrupt manner and her dislike of games. Later, recalling the cotton and bones figure of Comrade Pudinca to his American wife, he was astonished to hear that not all children learn the alphabet by standing up suddenly in unison with their eyes pinned to the symbols on the blackboard and shouting B! F! M! and so on. Discipline was Comrade Pudinca's big thing, the country's big thing at the time, and looking back he finds it amazing that he enjoyed these exercises.

His pleasure did not last very long.

Letters reminded him of people. Unlike numbers which were a thing in themselves with no particular visual feedback, letters looked exactly like Frau Weissmuler, Uncle Vlad, Granma, car conductors, classmates, milkmen, grocers and gypsies. L's, P's and S's were everywhere, sitting or standing, in groups of two or more, walking down the street or lingering in front of shop windows. If two lovers were sitting on a bench on his way back from school he would immediately see an A and a Z or an M. A syllable formed. Or a word. If they spelled AX, he would get scared and run. If they spelled AM he would look up at the big clock in the church tower to see if it was still morning. Buses were marvelous places filled with people sentences. Sometimes a whole bus would spell THERE IS A SNAKE UNDER YOUR SEAT or something equally ominous. As this faculty developed he could, deliberately, leave out some people to form very positive sentences

47

which then put him in a glorious frame of mind and he would arrive at school screaming, run into his classroom, throw his books on the desk and pull the girls' piggy tails and recite, breathlessly, such astonishing stories that the epithet "liar" seems to have been attached to him early.

His classmates were a bouquet of incongruity. Hardly any of them liked school. The few peasants who walked fifteen miles through the snow to get to school seemed to be the only exceptions. One in particular, Ion Vidrighin, wore bark shoes and cotton skirts and carried his books in a wool bag inside of which his mother had packed a large hunk of raw bacon, an onion and a loaf of black bread. This sumptuous fare was above what the rest ate and as a consequence, there was a great rush to be Ion's friend. Ion liked no one, however, and sat by himself on the cement steps leading to the former Mother Superior's office and sliced enormous chunks of bacon into neat squares with an evil looking razor-sharp shiv. Then he would put the onion on the higher step and smash it with his fist into a hundred pieces. "The power goes out of it this way," he said. Because of his razor, his taciturn manner and his oversized skeletal frame, Vidrighin commanded a great deal of respect. With his usual irreverent manner, Andrei Ivanovitch one day spilled a bottle of ink on the peasant's head during a totally silent sermon by the school principal. In the astonished silence that followed the stray giggles (he had hoped for a lot more!) the giant turned around and, without a word, planted his shiv in the desk. Everyone waited for the recess. This came soon enough, and the kids, expecting the worst, thickened around the two heroes. Searching his mind with feverish haste, Andrei Ivanovitch was beginning to shake a little. His phantom armies were not available. It would have taken too long to call Aunt Elena. He had to talk. And fast.
  –Do you know about lice? he said. The giant looked nonplussed. He was picking his teeth with his shiv.
  –Lice cover your head. I can see millions of lice on your head. Scattered laughter.
  –I poured the ink to get rid of the lice. The impertinence of the remark passed somehow over Vidrighin's head and, although

48

everyone was laughing, he began to search this very same head with a thoughtful hand. Lice, where he came from, were a real problem.

Later, alone with the giant, Andrei expressed in detail his great theory of lice. His concern impressed the peasant and soon, he had access to the slab of bacon and the red onion, to the pointed envy of everyone else.

"Everyone else" was a bunch of nondescript characters with closely shaven heads (regulation!), dressed in fragments of their parents' clothes, some military clothing was in evidence, and big clumsy shoes three sizes too big. This was a year before the introduction of school uniforms. These uniforms, coarse blue cotton, followed him for ten years.

Comrade Pudinca began to dislike him. She often made him stand up for no reason and go to a corner where he had to stay for the rest of the class. A great undeclared war developed between them. Even from his corner, though, he could always make one disruptive face. One day when she had thrown him out of the class altogether, he whistled in the hallway until she came out with a measuring stick and chased him all over the lugubrious corridors straight into the part of the building no one dared go into because it opened into the old church and led, through a series of rooms which were crowded with religious paraphernalia, into the funereal catacombs under the school.

Having found by mistake the entrance to the old church, he could think of nothing else for weeks. One morning he came to school early, armed with Uncle Vlad's priceless flashlight. He descended the stairway at the end of the corridor leading to the old church. At the bottom was a heavy metal door. He hesitated. Then, suddenly, he heard steps behind him. He turned around. Vidrighin, the giant, was coming toward him. He welcomed him in silence and, in marvelous unison, they proceeded to pull the door open. It was dark and musty inside and the flashlight barely made a small yellow spot on the limestone walls of the tunnel in front

49

of them. Encouraged, probably by a process of reverse bravery, they went in. On both sides of them the walls contained the graves of generations of nuns. The further they went in, the further back in time the graves went. A sister Paula, dead in 1879, would reappear fifty yards later, dead in 1636. The rows stretched into infinity, and names were scratched on the walls like teeth marks of a fabulous animal. They never got to the end of the tunnel. How could they have? No matter how many times they came back, there was always more, there were always new tunnels. These led, no doubt, under churches, homes and rivers to special, secret and forgotten shrines in the wilderness to which the older inhabitants of the city used to escape conquest, plagues and con-flagrations. Like all medieval cities, Sibiu was connected by a rich, albeit empty, underground system. In his deepest heart he knew that he too was built in the same way and that inside him there were the abandoned networks of extinct cultures.

As the taciturn Vidrighin led the way out of the underground, his thoughts had turned from fear to deep sadness. He felt sad for something he had never known. A beautiful friendship blossomed between the two. Vidrighin, who was trying to escape the predica-ment of his ancestors by going to school, knew even better than he did that all the stuff upstairs was bunk and this secret bound them together. All this, of course, is pure afterthought. Shivering there in the putrid old cemetery, he was probably more scared than anything else. And Vidrighin, although his friend, always seemed to him a sort of big dummy, which he no doubt was. All his friends, in fact, were dummies. He could not suffer anyone smarter than himself.

Learning to read in his second or third year was a lot more difficult. There is an impulse here to editorialize a little on this subject since it is of such objective importance, but we will refrain until we have taken a good look at little Ivanovitch being led out of school by his mother who has come to take him back to live with her. As always on these occasions, he was immensely grate-ful. The old gendarme was a good man and his obsessive measur-ing of his height in the doorway with a little knife had been really

50

helpful, but, alas, he didn't feel comfortable. His mother had remarried and when they got to his new house which was in the oldest section of town among towers and stairways, he was met at the door by a dark short man wearing a sleeveless shirt.

–So this is it, he said, bending down to examine him.

Purgu was a chemist and his hobby was making amateur radio sets. His workshop and his mother's bedroom were an exquisite mess of wires, tubes, printed patterns and technical manuals. At that time, Purgu had just begun work on a combination radio and tape recorder which was going to make him famous. Andrei's pleasure at seeing all of this stuff was soon dispelled by the man's stern order to stay out of the stuff or get his ass kicked.

This was no problem since, for the first time, he had his own room. This was a miracle of comfort in Rumania at a time when the housing crisis was very serious and often families crowded into small rooms with scores of relatives sharing every inch of space. Not only did he have his own room, but there was also a kitchen for their use only.

The bathroom, however, was down one flight of stairs. It had a rickety wooden door held by a latch from the inside. Aside from the discomfort of descending the stairs in the middle of the night, or in winter, the bathroom was *always* occupied. A curious dance of this period is the one foot shuffle which he practiced endlessly in front of the john waiting for Mr. Schmurtzvangel, the horrible old sausage maker on the third floor, to get out. After what seemed like ages, Schmurtzvangel would come out spitting, coughing and hoisting up his trousers, leaving a horrible smell of shit and cigar smoke behind. Young Ivanovitch would then crawl into the darkness of that stink pit and try, as hard as he could, to relieve himself. This, unfortunately, wasn't so easy because it involved a complete removal of the mind from the surroundings. The imagination compelled by those circumstances got so strong that it could transport him to Robinson Crusoe's island in a jiffy. But the place he most often visited in that place was a pirate's island with a hidden treasure on it. The search for the treasure

51

took anywhere from ten to twenty minutes and when he would finally get to it, his bowel movement would come out smooth and flawless, like china dolls.

Later, when asked how come most of his literary works last, when read out loud, from ten to twenty minutes, he shakes his head in total consternation. Does he or doesn't he know?

He and his mother's chemist didn't get along. Having learned, with great difficulty, how to read, he came home one day and wrote with great relish a few words on the white map of the world hanging in Purgu's room. These words he had just learned. They were: CUNT, COCK, SHIT, PISS, FUCK. He wrote them with a pencil and when he realized that he would most certainly get the strap for it, he hastened to erase them. But, damn it, the deep impression stayed even after trying everything to get it out including writing some new words on top. When Purgu came home from work he noticed the crime immediately. He burst out of the room and pulled Andrei in.
    –What did you write on the map?
    His mother wasn't home.
    –Nothing, he said.
    –You will eat nothing until you tell me the truth. Purgu, of course, could read the words perfectly well, but he had to elicit a confession.

His mother came home. She was shown the "crime" and converted to Purgu's point of view. A day and a night passed. He was starving. Next day, he smelled soup in the kitchen and could barely restrain himself from going in to ask Kiva, the old peasant maid, for some. But he didn't. The third day, he could barely stand up. At that point, he was pardoned against Purgu's will, and had a piece of bread. He felt transparent. He wasn't really hungry anymore. This was a beautiful angelic state. The phantoms from the Kodaly castle who hadn't been around in three years came back dressed in beautiful gold and silver clothes, with armor and white horses. His hunger had disappeared and it was only his mother's concern that got him to eat. With his stomach full, he

52

watched, regretfully, the world get thick again. He was hungry. He felt he had been cheated out of his magical world. He violently opened the door to Purgu's study and shouted as loud as he could:

–CUNT! COCK! SHIT! PISS! FUCK!

–Get out of here, little Jew, said the chemist.

6

A Jew.
  He was a Jew.
  What was a Jew?

One day, in class, when he just couldn't read the sentence, GA-
BRIEL IS PICKING FLOWERS, written neatly on the black-
board, Comrade Pudinca looked at him and said,
  –I thought Jews could read.

During breaks, there was always an inevitable fight (which, with
the help of Vidrighin, he always won) that ended up with the
word JEW! thrown at him like a stone. But with this, Vidrighin
could not help him, because Vidrighin wasn't a Jew.

He would shake his fists furiously at the disappearing creature but
could find no word he could shout back. He would have liked to
shout JEW! back, but he knew that the others weren't Jews and
he could not think of any word that was the opposite of Jew in
maleficence because he did not know what a Jew was, nor did he
want to ask anybody. It seemed inconceivable to him that his
mother would know. Only his father would know. But he was
dead.
  –There goes the little Jew, said the man at the candy store.

There was another Jew in school, a small shy creature who could
not speak Rumanian very well. He had long sideburns curling
around his face and was also the butt of countless cruel pranks.

Andrei never felt as if he should go to his defense because it would have implied his own consent to the fact of being a Jew. So, instead, he participated (with some painful reserve) in pulling the boy's whiskers and sticking his tongue out at him. This made him feel uneasy. One day, he walked up to the lonely figure. His name was Berl.

–Would you like to walk home from school with me? he said.

They walked. Berl seemed to know what a Jew was. He received an invitation to go and visit Berl behind the old Jewish synagogue where he lived. He politely declined this invitation and promptly forgot all about it.

The phys. ed. teacher was a square-looking, stupid peasant who tortured Andrei endlessly. His name was Cobza which means Violin, and Cobza was anything but. He had a hoarse voice and a brutal manner. He loved to single him out in the morning, make him step out of the line, and point out, with smug satisfaction, how skinny his legs were and what a curious nose he had. After these deliveries he would make him do forty pushups on one hand, walk upside down on the parallel bars, run fifty times around the gym, etc. One time he singled him out and said:

–Goldmutter, Goldshitter, what kind of a name is that?

Yes, his name. What about his name? What does Goldmutter mean? Gold Mother. Excuse me, Sun, I didn't mean it, but what's this "gold mother" all about? He said nothing.

–WHAT ARE YOU ANYWAY? snarled Cobza. The class sniggered.

–I'M A BASTARD, SIR! he answered, and his answer carried the day because everyone was laughing with him at Cobza who stood, flushed, in the middle of the gym. It was no victory, though. The war was just beginning.

He went to visit Berl.

The old Spanish-style synagogue was falling to pieces. He passed through a melancholy looking wrought iron gate, walked up the mossy brick path and headed toward the back. He didn't know why, but he was afraid. The fading Jewish letters on the frontispiece glowed ominously even though it was only four in the afternoon and summertime at that. The place smelled peculiar, pleasant, but not familiar.

Berl was in the kitchen. His mother greeted Ivanovitch effusively. There must not have been many visitors of her son's age. She was making some kind of round balls of dough with a glove, dropping them in a boiling pot. The association with Ilse's chicken soup made him recoil.

Berl showed him the mysterious building. There was a decaying swimming pool with marble steps in one of the rooms, filled with greenish water. In the main hall, the chairs were all cushioned with dark old velvet torn in places, and the tubular gold Torah behind a pulpit covered with a fringed purple brocade, glowed at him.

To his relief, he was soon taken out of there and they went into a big barn where, among grass growing through the boards, was the supple and enormous body of the synagogue hearse, a horse-drawn affair without horses, on which they climbed and played until the sun set.

Having stayed for dinner, he was surprised to find that he enjoyed the chicken soup with the balls in it. Before dinner he met Berl's father, a mustachioed little man whom he liked instantly. Samuel, as he was known, gave him something to cover his head with and mumbled some remote words. After dinner, Berl's father began questioning him.

–Do you know anything about your people, Goldmutter?

–No, sir.

–Your grandfather was a grand old crook, Goldmutter, but a good Jew, don't you forget it. They used to have the synagogue meetings in the back of his old tent full of trinkets during the war. And your grandmother, boy, she had a heart of gold. She used to come here and sit with us behind the old synagogue where we trembled every day in fear for our lives, and prayed to the Lord for the days of our lives, and she would bring Yamala cold borscht and chicken paprikash and bring news of your father who was running around with the partisans. She was so worried about him. He wasn't a good Jew, she said. He became a Communist. I'm

56

not so sure about Julius not being a good Jew, though . . . If it wasn't for him, this old house of prayer wouldn't be standing today, so help us God . . . When he and his cronies blew up that Müller sonofabitch and his old Kommandatur, that was the last we heard from the Germans about pulling down this building.

Samuel went on in this manner for hours until he noticed that it was dark outside. He put on his coat and took young Goldmutter home. His mother opened the door. She was astonished to see the strange pair.

–Where have you been? she said. I was hysterical.

Without inviting Samuel into the house, she pulled him in and closed the door.

–I was a Jew, he said.

–Don't let Purgu hear you, said Mother. For Godssake, boy, you could be arrested for talking to that old Jew.

He didn't go back to Berl's for a long time. They would see each other in school and they would greet each other cautiously. But one day they fell into step together as they were going toward their respective homes.

–Do you want to come? said Berl.

–Yes.

The room with the swimming pool in it looked surprisingly clean and sunny. The water also looked clean and in it he saw a number of boys he had never met, some his age, some older.

–These are my cousins, Berl said, they live in Alba Iulia. They came to visit us. It turned out that all of them knew Aunt Elena from around town.

–Take off your clothes and jump in, said Berl, doing just that.

He felt a little shy, and would have never jumped into the pool if he had known beforehand that one of the boys was not a boy at all but a girl. When he became aware of his mistake, he blushed deeply and remembered Vera, the little girl under the piano. He tried as hard as he could not to look at what was most certainly a pretty little mound with a tiny crack in it, and started splashing

57

around, seemingly unconcerned. But the time came, finally, when he could restrain himself no longer and looked straight at it. An electric warmth went through him. Everyone noticed. "Look," said Berl, and he took his little circumcised thing which was just like his own and was, in addition, hard, and he rubbed it right smack against the girl's crack. The girl giggled with pleasure. From that moment on, Andrei wanted to do nothing more than that.

—Do you want to do it? she said to him and to him only. He knew that she wanted him to.

—No, he said.

He regrets this NO more than anything in his life. Even now he lies on his back in dark rooms and his imagination changes that No into a YES, a process which has gone on for twenty years and will go on for twenty more.

When he went home that night he was in a daze. He was again worried about being late, but somehow it didn't matter. At his street corner he saw two bigger boys, whom he knew, standing in a doorway with their hands deep in their pockets.

—Come here, one of them said.

Thinking it was important, he went over. Both of them had their soft pizzles out of their pants and were pissing toward each other in a crosswise fashion.

—What? he said.

—Every time two people piss like this, a Jew dies, said the bigger of the two.

7

School rolled on in pathetic absurdity. At home, he started building a library and drawing pirates. He took large sheets of white paper and filled them with boats full of pirates fighting in two dimensions. The nature of these pirate drawings was such that if any white showed in the drawing he hastened to put two tiny pirates in it. He filled the page to exhaustion and uninitiated observers could have, possibly, counted 20 pirates on a page when there were actually 300, hidden in every recess. The books were all adventure books, Robinson Crusoe, the Dumas stories, Gulliver, and one or two funny books, including *Three Men in a Boat* by some English author, the funniest book he has ever read.

Purgu had gone completely insane over a new type of photo-radio that took pictures during songs, so Andrei saw very little of him, which was all to the best.

Dinner time, though, was a nightmare.
   Kiva, the maid, was eighty years old and everything she cooked had tons of fried and boiled onions in it. Just the words "cooked onion" make him cringe still. All would have gone well, however, if Purgu hadn't gotten it through his head that he ought to make Andrei eat everything on the plate. For a while, the child used every trick to get away from dinner. Headaches, stomachaches, school, etc. When these failed, he began palming pieces of meat and putting them in his pants, or pouring spoonfuls of stew onto the floor.
   –What did you just do? said Purgu. He confessed.

59

–Kiva, fill his plate. Kiva did. The stuff was a green paste with fried onions in it.

–Now eat it.

He began. But there was no way to finish it. He felt the little nudges of nausea gathering in clumps in his throat. Purgu bent over him.

–EAT!

He shook his head negatively. Purgu took the spoon out of his hand and said:

–OPEN YOUR MOUTH!

He did. But instead of the emptiness Purgu expected, the thick green stuff welled up from the recesses of his stomach and came out in great gushes all over Purgu's hands, all over Purgu's lemon-colored brand-new pants, and all over Purgu's shoes.

Dinner time became slightly more bearable because Purgu would not chance ruining another suit of clothes, but Kiva's cooking stayed the same.

Every morning at seven o'clock, he got up, combed his hair straight over his head as far away from his forehead as he could (Aunt Elena once told him that hair would grow from his forehead if he didn't comb it straight up), and took off for school.

The street, particularly in the winter, was dark, and groups of people waited at the trolley station to go to work. Before leaving, he always had café au lait and a piece of bread and butter, and for lunch Kiva had wrapped a bacon-grease sandwich with paprika in his school case. He was one of the first to arrive in school and the first to leave. Numerous teachers had been added and now he was, in addition to reading and writing, studying history and arithmetic. These two subjects were fascinating and his grades in arithmetic were excellent. History, which he liked, was taught by a complete idiot with thick glasses, Comrade Bratu, who always brought a school text with him and read lessons out of it without a single word of comment. He had his reasons, no doubt. The textbook was new and it contained history just rewritten from the Marxist point of view and since he was an old teacher used to teaching history in other ways, he thought better than to take any chances. Even so, through the pages of the Marxist textbook laden with clichés, Andrei could glimpse a fascinating vista of characters. He loved historical characters because no matter what their actions, they seemed to be always interesting. Nobody he knew was possessed of any greatness, with the possible exception of the two baronesses in Alba Iulia, but he hadn't seen them for years. Everyone else was stupid, mean and petty.

In reading, Madame Pudinca (who was still with him) brought poems to class. All these poems belonged to a class of heroic times when words were not valued for their natural uses but rather for the extravagant sonority of their vowels. Alecsandri, the worst of Eminescu and tons of George Cosbuc were poured into his naive mind. Not that he didn't love them. To stand erect in front of a field of newly liberated serfs, put one hand in his shirt and declare in rhyme that "the world is seeing golden dawns and flowers sweet," as Alecsandri had, was no mean thing. Secretly he still preferred adventure stories to waves of rhetoric but he saw no contradiction, really. Rhetoric was the high point of adventure, the point when one unveiled one's heroism in public. He became very good at recitation. He was always chosen, out of his class, to recite at year's end, the poem "Mother" by Cosbuc, a poem which never failed to bring tears to all eyes. Poor mother, all alone and abandoned through the whole poem, keeps looking out the darkened windows for a sign of her son. He doesn't come.

It would never have occurred to him to start writing this kind of stuff if it hadn't been for dinnertime at home. It was one of his excuses for not coming to dinner.
　　—I have to write a poem for school!
　　He remembers his first poem or, at least, the way it came about. He was sitting at the kitchen table, full of ideas about a poem of praise to the Socialist Republic of Rumania. Like Cosbuc's poem, he wanted his poem to bring tears to all concerned. He was overflowing with patriotism. Mother was sitting across the table on the divan, knitting or polishing her fingernails.
　　—What rhymes with country?

61

–Pantry, said Mother.
–With bless?
–Stress.
And so on, my sweet country, you who are a full pantry. Don't forget to bless us under stress, or thereabouts. Then it all came together. The mice found the ice, the night found the light.

The effect of this first quatrain was shattering. Mother called in every conceivable neighbor.

–Tell us, she said when they all gathered, how will she bless us under stress?

Fat Butuc was there (with the soup spoon still in his mouth), Madame Pia with her sewing, the two Gypsy brothers, Grigore and Smitan, the railroad light man with coal on his face, etc. To these and more he told his poem. Great gasps of disbelief came from the audience.

–He copied it out of a book, said Fat Butuc.
–It's not possible, said the brothers in unison.
–He's only ten years old, chirped Madame Pia.

In school, the effect was just as large, if not as effusive. He was a poet.

Beginning now, his head was always full of odes to his sweet country although he suspected that tears in all eyes was his real intention and that his sweet country was merely a formality for bringing out the tears. He and his mother worked as a team. He would find the ideas, she would find the rhymes. And it is in this way that things still stand. He finds the ideas and Mother finds all the rhymes, the form.

Poetry had invaded his life earlier too. Grandmother loved to tell rhymed sentimental poems which were the texts of songs she couldn't sing because her voice would crack. Later, he heard bawdy poems in school and on the street and could recite quite a number of them, without an idea of what they meant. And then he started making up his own bawdy poems because dirty words rhymed so easily. To think that any of the acts described in these had anything to do with life was absurd.

62

During the summer he went to a pioneer camp in the mountains directly above Sibiu. The mighty Carpathian range excited him as nothing had before. He had never been this close to the jagged peaks he used to see out his window and of which he had been incessantly dreaming. The camp was in a beautiful clearing at very high altitude. The camp had been the prize for having won a recitation contest in school with the poem "Mother" by Cosbuc. He was, frankly, very tired of that poor woman. He was, after all, ten and a half. He ran through the woods all summer but the nights around the campfire were the most beautiful of all. Singing went on and the girls and the boys sat very close together, sometimes touching, and, most of all, he remembers a skinny blonde girl with a crooked smile, a short navy blue skirt, two tanned legs, and that is all he remembers. One evening a boy named Militaru, which means Military, asked him to compare sizes. They went to the side, into a little clump of bushes where they could still see clearly because the moon was out. He pulled his out of his pants. It was hard. Militaru pulled out his and, true to his name, it was of a truly magnificent military size, a cannon. This, Andrei Ivanovitch found hard to believe since he had always thought that the thing in his shorts was enormous. They got their two pricks really close together and he looked some more, his once-powerful member looking timid next to the proud hardness of the other's. Militaru touched his prick with his. It felt good. They did this for awhile until they were both flushed in the face. Later, that night Militaru came to his bed and they both held each other's while Militaru told him how babies were made. The boy, he said, puts his in the girl's crack and boom comes Baby. This he could not quite believe. The camp was situated at the edge of some ancient Roman baths fallen into ruin and, next day, Militaru promised that he would show him with a girl if he stayed quietly behind a tree and didn't say a word. He waited all night for it but when nobody showed up he went back to bed. He thought a lot about this. Camp was almost over and the image of Boom comes Baby and what went on before was on his mind. Back home, he decided to test his newly found knowledge by repeating it to the younger boy on the floor below. Hans was horrified. He listened to the whole story, then went home and told his mother. Frau Gramm was fat and excitable. She opened the door to their apartment almost without breathing and exploded into a series of gruesome predicaments:

–That boy (meaning Ivanovitch) will end up a bum, take my word for it, Frau Purgu.

After Frau Gramm had gone, his mother took him gently by the hand and told him to sit down. He was terrified because he was sure that the secret knowledge he had revealed carried severe penalties if bandied about. But his mother, in one of her rare acts of reasonableness, spoke thus:

–Frau Gramm is a fat old bitch. If you know about these things then you shouldn't tell them to Hans because he is a stupid little boy.

My God! Not only was there no penalty but it was all true! He couldn't wait to make a baby. But first he had to put it in. He began looking at his classmates with different eyes. He imagined the whole thing and, Boom comes Baby!

Olga Pitic (Dwarf) seemed interested. After endless days of preliminaries, they agreed to meet after school in the back and go down a special door into the tunnel where the nuns were buried.

Olga Pitic laughed a lot and exuded an unmistakable sexuality which was like a strong drug. It enveloped her from the tips of her toes through her plump thighs barely hidden by the school dress to the tip of her nose which was little and turned up. She came as far as the door to the tunnel but refused to go on.

–Don't you want to see the dead nuns? he said, disappointed.

Mysteriously, she took his hand and guided it under her dress and put it on her mound. His fingers were trembling with excitement. Then he felt her crack with his finger and was lost. Olga unbuttoned his pants and caressed his. Eternities passed. They agreed to meet again next day in the same place.

Tomorrow, he thought, tomorrow. Boom goes Baby. Boom went his heart.

But tomorrow never came because that day Purgu had received immediate orders from the company for which he worked to present himself without delay to a remote industrial development in the western part of Transylvania. Without saying goodbye to anyone, they shipped out in the morning. Luggage and possessions had been arranged for by Kiva. They were due in a week.

There was a sense of emergency in the air. Everyone on the train seemed preoccupied. Purgu said nothing and kept his head in his hands. Mother looked out the window. The magnificent Carpathians loaded with autumn rolled by. The train was hypnotic. The Hungarian Revolution had broken out across the border.

8

Until 1954 only the shepherds and their sheep disturbed the peace in these mountains. Then came Victory City, a chemical plant surrounded by shacks. It was still mostly a makeshift operation when they got there. Endless wooden barracks stretched out in rows of one hundred, concentrically from the central square. The chemical plant belched purple smoke from a hill directly across the town. Victory City was modeled after its counterparts in Siberia and thus many political exiles worked at the plant. All the people there were, in fact, considered to have run West or East of the Communist Party line. This is why internal security was a vast operation in Victory City. There was one informer per six persons. Outside the plant, life revolved around the central square with the statue of Karl Marx in the middle of it. Here was a place for talk for the people who worked the night shift and a place for gossip and romance for those who worked the day shift. Since everyone worked, the wives and the husbands were, as a rule, on opposite shifts and thus a lot of affairs were going on counter-shift. There was a rotation system,too, which made a vast lottery out of people's time. Most of the people were young, and children no bigger than Ivanovitch constituted the town majority.

Purgu, being a chemical engineer, was part of the better class of people in town because, incredible as it may seem, class distinction was an obsession here. The engineers and commissars were the better people. And the engineers were there to be watched by the commissars. Together, they all watched the workers.

Their barracks was green and there were two beds in it. He slept in the one close to the door; mother and Purgu slept in the other. There was a table and an umbrella, a clothes rack, a loose board behind which they hid their gun, and there was a tiny window. When they settled in the cabin, mother acquired a radio from somewhere. And the Hungarian revolution came into the room. They could see the Hungarian border from where they were living so that whenever listening to the radio, Andrei would turn his head in that direction. He could see, almost taste, the smoke and flames. The whole town was looking in that direction. The Hungarian radio stations were coming in clearly and one afternoon the excitement peaked. Imre Nagy was speaking when there was a burst of gunfire which, on the radio, sounded like a buzz of wild mosquitoes. Another voice came through almost immediately and told everyone to go home and put down the guns because the Soviets were in control. During the last part of the broadcast there was some more machine-gun fire and yet a third voice began speaking. The Russian tanks were burning, the third voice said, and the Communists and Jews will all burn in a matter of days.

This was exciting. They stayed up all night listening. There were rumors at the plant next day that the students in Cluj, not far from where they were, had started erecting barricades and that Molotov cocktails were flying on the streets. The revolution was going to spread. Little groups of people gathered everywhere in nervous clumps. Chief of Internal Security, Colonel Sasz, ordered a few arrests. Colonel Sasz was in a peculiar position. He was Hungarian and, in his heart, he supported the revolution but he worked for the Rumanian militia and had to constantly prove his loyalty. Transylvania was a bed of thorns. At the end of the Second World War, the last set of Transylvanian ping-pong had been played. Stalin had taken it from the Hungarians (whom he hated more than anyone else) and gave it back to the Rumanians in whose possession it had been before Hitler (who loved the Hungarians) had given it to the Hungarians. The question had never been left to the Transylvanians.

Colonel Sasz and Mother were friends. The colonel's two sons, a freckled pair of identical twins, took Andrei up into the mountains and showed him paths. They had been there since the beginning of Victory City and they knew the mountains better than anyone else. In the evening, they all gathered around the radio in the colonel's room and listened to the forbidden Hungarian radio stations. The broadcasts were interrupted only by Colonel Sasz's sighs of sympathy followed immediately by his mumbled denial of sympathy with those "savages."

–Duty is duty, he mumbled sadly.

It got worse. The Russians, it seemed, were in control in most places. The Cluj rebellion had fizzled out. There was still isolated fighting but the big rush of the first days had passed. But Andrei's mind was seething with images. He had heard stories of twelve-year-old children, his age, throwing Molotov cocktails at Russian tanks. The ceaseless nighttime radio listening had sharpened his perception to a point. Discipline, suddenly relaxed, allowed him to roam the empty streets at night, machine gun in hand, performing various heroic acts. There was a curfew on. It was dangerous. One rainy night, holding a piece of chalk in his sweaty hand, he scribbled LONG LIVE THE REVOLUTION! in huge, childish letters on the side of a wooden partition around a construction site. He knew he would be in trouble if caught, colonel or no colonel. He couldn't sleep the rest of that night impatient for the day when he could see the effect of his courageous statement. Would the workers rise? Last night's rain had washed it away!

Suddenly, there was silence. The revolution was over. Mother Russia licked her paws. Millions were dead, thousands had run away. Andrei Ivanovitch wandered through the nearby mountains, thinking. He didn't know what the revolution had been about, he did not know the depths from which it had sprung, he knew nothing and yet he felt sad as if a personal loss had taken place. He had no way of knowing that he was an addict to revolution, that it ran in his blood. As he pondered this he was walking in the same mountains his father had, when, as a partisan, he was hiding from the Nazis at the beginning of the war. One day, Andrei's wanderings took him to a small overgrown military cemetery. The square stones had Jewish letters on them. He imagined that a battle had taken place there. His father's regiment had been wiped out and Father had escaped, alone, by scaling the sheer cliff of the Suru Mountain. He acted and re-enacted this scene.

Purgu, who had just perfected a radio set that could count money, was sent by the factory to Bucharest to purchase some materials. The colonel came often during the absence. Now that all was quiet on the other side of the border, he had released arrested men and women, but his brooding hadn't left him. After he would leave, Mother (thinking that Andrei was asleep) pried open the board on the wall and took out the gun. It was a monumental Russian revolver. She held it for a few minutes, then she put it back. He thought of all the dangers. There didn't seem to be any. The purple smoke from the factory curled into the stars.

In Victory City, the city of a million clotheslines and a million bread lines (not to speak of meat lines which ran into infinity with even the slightest rumor of pork chops arriving), he acquired a great love for the mountains. The Carpathian range started outside the window and went straight up into the sky as far as he could see. In the winter, that *particular* winter, it was covered with a deep clean layer of snow. All the tense and bright images created by the revolution had, for background and color, these fierce mountains, and he saw brutal little colonels with pockmarked faces climbing up the purple smoke of the chemical plant into the white immensity. The colonels, it seems, were defending the plant against the mountain and if he looked up, really high up, he could see the snowstorms of invisible battles.

He smoked his first cigarette.
One of the colonel's sons, Gyuri, watched him choke.
–If you don't give me all your stamps, I'll tell your mother you smoked a cigarette, he said.
Andrei had a beautiful stamp collection, started back in Sibiu.

There were only new stamps in the collection and he spent days at the time studying them through a magnifying glass.

–No.

As he said he would, Gyuri told Andrei's mother. Mother slapped her son wildly across the face and sent him to the barber, a supreme punishment in those days. The barbershop was across the "street" in a green shack. He watched his hair being shorn in the mirror. And then, to make matters worse, Purgu arrived from Bucharest, having failed to purchase materials for the plant and having failed, also, to convince anyone of the merits of his cash register radio. In this mood, Purgu confiscated his stamp collection and sold it to a miserable old man who collected rags, bottles, and cigarette butts, for a mere five leis.

–You spend too much time with it and not enough time in school, he said.

Andrei walked about, for the next two days, deeply immersed in his revenge. Purgu's body, pierced through and through with the broken bottles of the old wretch, twitched in agony. The body of the ragpicker, filled to the teeth with Purgu's cash register radio, bled on the snow. His stamps, glued all over the mutilated bodies of the two, made neat human packages. But it wasn't enough! He had to *do* something. Twelve-year-old Hungarian children had thrown Molotov cocktails! He had a plan. A couple of weeks before, he had found a warm creek bed in the back of the plant. This creek bed was covered with a deposit of waste from the plant. The waste consisted mostly of bright little pellets which burned like sparklers and could, if enough of them were gathered, blow a huge stone ten feet across. Andrei gathered two pickle jars full.

That night, he crept out of the house with three matchboxes packed tight with the explosive. In each matchbox he put a long piece of string soaked in kerosene. A fourth matchbox was left behind under Purgu's invention. The fuse to the fourth box was in his hand. He put another box under the door of the barbershop and tied the two fuses together. He lit them and ran. He was running so fast that he was already on the outer perimeter of Victory City when he heard the explosions. Boom, boom, booom.

70

He was still running, later, when he found himself on the donkey road leading over the Suru Mountain. The road was covered with snow, there were no fresh tracks and the night was clear. The moon and the stars were out. He was still holding the remaining two matchboxes in his hand. He looked at these for a moment and then threw them as far as he could into the snow. He wasn't going back.

He found the Jewish cemetery without difficulty. He had gone there so many times in the fall. He didn't know why he'd gone there but as he stood staring at the bright frozen snow, he felt that his father was there. Silently, he asked his father if it was all right to run away. Yes, his father said. It is OK every time. Then, just as quietly, his father advised him which paths to take. Father was speaking very slowly, very very clearly. Take the straight road over the Capra Cliff, he said, and keep on it until you get to the Dobra Stones, the ones that look like old women crying. Five meters to the left of the biggest one, who looks as if her hair is flying in the wind, stop. There is a storehouse there.

The snow was deep but frozen over. He felt an uncanny knowledge of the paths. As he walked, his shoes squeaked plaintively. He knew the Capra Cliff well from the fall. It was a steep donkey path going straight over the mountain. He walked fiercely and, as he did, he began to sweat. He had two sweaters on and his long windbreaker on top of these. There were sounds coming from the belly of the mountain, deep, grave sounds, and he could also hear a lone wolf once in a while. Walk, walk, walk. Stumble, stumble, stumble.

It was almost dawn and he was sleepwalking when he got to the Dobra Stones. The old women looked frightening. Their twisted stone bodies, sitting in a circle, told a tragic story. The biggest one, who looked as if her grief had torn her limb from limb without killing her, towered way above the others. It was the one Father had spoken of. He walked what he thought were five meters to the left of it. There was nothing there, only snow. He started to dig, painfully, one inch at a time. He was very tired and

71

the snow was hard. Don't fall asleep, said Father. He didn't or maybe he did because by now his hands moved of themselves and he was numb.

Suddenly, there was a smooth square stone. He pulled at it. This stone weighed, to be sure, more than a ton. But he was getting help. Right alongside him, a giant arm was tensing under the weight. When the stone was off, he saw a hole going somewhere into the earth. A few stairs went in. It began to snow lightly. He descended carefully on all fours, feeling his way as light snowflakes fell after him into the ditch. He was now inside a neat little room. Against the walls, he could make out rows of frozen rifles, like people sleeping. Or were they people sleeping? There was also a shelf full of cans, a pile of bayonets and a bed. He fell on it.

When he woke the sun was straight up in the sky and he was covered with a layer of snow. He opened a can with a bayonet and ate the stuff inside. It didn't taste too bad. Well, it was food anyhow. Not until later, in America, did he taste anything like that. It was Spam and it occurred to him that this was the place the partisans were heading to when they had been surprised by the Germans, and that the Spam must have been parachuted to the partisans by a British or American plane. He ate three of those cans. It was daytime now and he knew that from where he was he could easily reach Paltza, a summer resort on the other side of the Dobra Stones. He reached Paltza in the late afternoon.

The astonished elderly couple who took care of the resort and wintered there, could not believe their eyes. Nobody could get there in the winter, they said. Nobody. The donkey path was treacherous, unusable. It was a wonder of the world. Incredible. Using an old crank telephone, they called Victory City. The operator located his mother at the plant, where she was taking photographs, and called her to the phone. Mother was in tears. She could hardly talk. The whole damn town had nearly burnt down. What had he done? Then, Mother went on to say, when the fire was put out she realized that he was gone, she had been afraid that he was dead. How did Mother know what he had done? She had found pellets, that's how. Luckily, no one was hurt. After some more tears, she added that she loved him and he should come home. He felt terrible.

But there was no way for him to go home until spring, a full two months away. A party of ten men and dogs was needed to get him off the mountain. No one had the time. He cried a bit but, deep inside, he felt good.

And that is where he spent the winter after the Hungarian revolution, picking roots under the snow, helping the old couple sweep up, and telling amazing stories about himself. The kind old folks believed everything he told them because how could one not believe a boy who had, all alone, scaled the Capra in winter?

9

–How old are you, boy?

–Fourteen.

–You're lying. You couldn't be more than eleven.

–Whatever.

–Why were you beating on the telephone with your fists?

–The dime wouldn't come out.

–Wasn't it because you wanted *all* the dimes to come out? How old are you?

–Fourteen.

–If you're lying about your age, and you *are*, you are most certainly lying about the telephone. You were robbing a public telephone. You come with me.

The man grabbed him as he was about to sprint.

In the back room of the police station, six forlorn Gypsies were all screaming at the same time, denying vehemently something highly unclear.

–What kind of a boy are you? said the chief, caressing his empty holster.

–A Jew, sir.

–That figures. Get him out of here, Stan, and don't you ever be so stupid again to arrest a Jew for an untypical crime. Jews don't rob telephones. They steal gold.

When the policeman said "gold," Andrei's heart sank. How did that policeman know? Just the day before, he had broken into his school (which lay quietly in the smoldering heat because it was summertime), and had stolen the school's coin collection, a big wooden box filled with silver and gold coins, mostly Roman. This collection had been assembled by the nuns in the days of yore and the school had inherited it. The box just lay on a shelf in the chemistry laboratory. He had been attracted to it, irresistibly, ever since he had discovered it. After lowering himself into the lab through the window and out of it through a sewer, he'd taken the box home and spread the contents on the bed. There was nobody to be afraid of. He was alone with Kiva who was very old and blind. Mother had stayed behind in Victory City and he had returned to Sibiu, a day after his thirteenth birthday, to spend the summer.

Yes, there certainly was something about gold. He rubbed the lumpy Roman coins until his hands were sweaty. Old Baron Kodaly walked swiftly and unnoticeably through the room, jingling gold chains, flashing a mouthful of gold, rubbing a round gold belly watch, while, a little ahead of him, Grandfather Goldmutter juggled enormous light balls of gold saying, Now you see it! Now you don't! The policeman was right. Jews hoarded gold. Jews loved gold. Every week there was another arrest of a Jew with a stash of gold under his floor. There goes old Leibowitz, Mother used to say, as they watched a shivering old man being dragged out of his house in his nightclothes by cockroach-colored police with rifles.

Rumania is mostly an Oriental country so it's not only Jews struck by the fever. The main supply of the country's gold is in the hands of the Russians and there exists a psychic "gold vacuum" which anybody on the street experiences in the form of a lack of oxygen. Having more Gypsies than anywhere else in Europe, there is a lot more gold mythology to go around, because Gypsies, who have been known to distrust the official currencies of states ever since their beginnings, change everything of value into gold. Add to this the fact that the Communists, hard as they tried to deny it, had gold on their minds. Take, for example, the typical description of Communism in school books: "The golden future of humanity!" Fairy tales which have no gold in them are fabrications.

75

Ivanovitch glanced at the bookshelf. There at the end of it was VOLUME ONE of his masterpiece. VOLUME ONE, as was written in large letters on the cardboard cover of the lined notebook, contained the adventures of a small boy who hides in an empty barrel aboard a ship with the stated destination "America." Soon, however, it becomes apparent that it is not to America that the ship is going. After two days of travel, the French flag is lowered and the pirate flag is raised on the mast. The little boy, tortured by hunger, presents himself to the captain of the ship who orders him thrown overboard. "Wait," the boy says, "is there anyone here courageous enough to fight me?" The men and the captain laugh. Finally a huge hunk of brutal meat steps forward. "Fight *him!*" laughs the third class steward. The boy draws back, and, suddenly . . . a ship has been sighted. Everyone runs back to their duties. Later, the girl with the golden hair . . . but wait, the notebook just ended and VOLUME TWO hasn't yet been written.

The girl with the golden hair wasn't his sole property. Every romantic tale or tale worth its flights had her in it. Who was she? Aside from his book, which was proceeding very slowly (much, much slower than his other notebook, entitled OBSERVA-TIONS, which was almost full), he began looking at all the girls on the street and in the parks where he wandered all day. For awhile he was madly in love with a golden girl called Lemon, who used to sit in a swing in Bruckenthal Park sucking her fingernails, surrounded by a crowd of male admirers. His imagination was fired when one of the boys reported to him that Lemon "kissed me in the bushes." For two weeks, the burning problem of intro-ductions tortured him. After discarding several romantic a la Dumas-type greetings such as, "What is my fair lady seeing in the pink horizon?", he decided to go straight to the core of the situation which was (as he saw it) to show her how much more interesting *he* was than the boy whom she had allegedly kissed in the bushes. So, he walked up to her one afternoon, walking awk-wardly, as befit a swordsman, and began his tale:
—When I was in China . . .
This is all he said. A chorus of laughter, including his Lemon's,

met him. Feeling deeply the ridiculousness of his position, he turned his eyes toward a point in the distance, as if he had meant to address someone else altogether (a cloud, perhaps), and walked straight past the group. There is no doubt, they thought he was weird. But today, with all this gold, today he did not care. He could buy a castle and Lemon would come crying to him.

Meanwhile, a minor rebellion was brewing in town. It seems that some workers at the BOBINA started to tear down the Oval Cemetery to build houses there, a project which did not have the sanction of the Health Ministry.

The Oval, one of the many cemeteries of Sibiu abandoned in the eighteenth century after the plague, contained splendid rundown tombs and crypts of Transylvanian nobility and was full of mysterious whispering spirits. He was deadly afraid of the place because, a few weeks before, he had fallen into an open grave. He had been running through the place, as usual, past the Mausoleum of Baron Von Bruckenthal (inside of which he and Peter and Radu had smoked cigarettes, flipping their ashes philosophically over the marble angels holding urns), past the two rows of weeping willows behind which life-size statues of knights in armor stood at attention, past the Rokaczi family monuments of bizarre scenes from the Apocalypse and the Resurrection in black marble. And as soon as he had gone past these, he tripped, fell, and was flying through the mouth of an open grave. He landed, fifteen feet later, with a horrible crrrrakkk on a putrid something in two feet of water. The experience, after he had crawled out by grabbing handfuls of grass growing through the walls, had left him scared of the place. But rumors of something going on at the Oval overrode his fear, and, without thinking, Andrei filled his pockets with stolen Roman gold and headed for the place.

Nobody on the streets. The oppressive heat of summer afternoon kept everyone indoors. He loved the heat, the sensual action of the sun. On the way to the Oval he was thinking of Lemon. As he left the last houses and shops behind, he had the actual feeling of the girl sitting next to him. She "kissed him in the bushes."

77

His cock stiffened. It was awkward walking as long as the deliciousness of Lemon enveloped him. He took it out of his pants and walked straight across an abandoned field, following it like a finger pointing the direction. It had a will of its own. The sun beat down and he was red all over. Where was it taking him? He was some ten or fifteen feet from the Oval when he saw people near the gate. He quickly stuffed the thing, which had become enormous, into his pants, and looking seemingly unconcerned, headed for the group.

Radu, who was also thirteen (an escapee from a state home who lived in the cemetery), was among the people. He was in the annoying habit of always calling Ivanovitch "punk."

–They've started work around here, punk, so I hefta move soon!

–The workers are building themselves houses, punk, and they say the Party's all excited. . . .

The rest of the crowd seemed to be relatives of the workers inside. By their talk, it seemed that they were waiting for something to happen. "The project had his approval," said a fat woman and everyone nodded. "He" was, no doubt, Secretary Rana of the local Communist Party.

Then, suddenly, a military jeep pulled in, in a cloud of dust.

There were three soldiers with machine guns in it. A sweating, corpulent man sitting in front, dressed in suit and tie, stood up and bellowed through the mouth of a loudspeaker mounted on the back of one of the soldiers:

–By order of the Health Ministry, I summon you to stop working on this site immediately!

–Hell's gonna break loose, punk. . . .

The angry workers poured out of the cemetery, waving their picks and axes.

–We need houses. I got six children and ten relatives in one room!

–My mother is eighty years old and has no bed of her own!

The fat man stood wincing, listening to all this, wiping his forehead with a checkered handkerchief.

–If there are any questions, you go and ask Secretary Rana about it, he said.

The men had a short angry conference. The project had had the Secretary's implicit agreement. He had promised.
–LET'S GO!
–Let's go, punk, said Radu.
The two of them followed the men and the jeep followed all of them from a short distance. It was a hot, silent walk.

–We want to see Comrade Rana, shouted the men when they arrived at the square.
Passersby stopped and demanded to know what the issue was. Soon, they too began to shout. The jeep stood immobile in one corner of the square. The crowd was thickening.
–Watch your feet, punk, advised Radu, who, as a veteran of official encounters, knew the best way to deal with them. He was ready to sprint.
Some bricks and stones, torn from the square, started flying at the windows of the Party Headquarters. This is when he followed Radu's advice, running as fast as he could out of the square. He learned later that as soon as the first shower of glass had hit the pavement the soldiers on the jeep had opened machine-gun fire.

He was safe on the platform of the tramway crawling up the hill, which both he and Radu had boarded in full movement. They stayed on the iron ramp at the back of the tramway all the way to the lower station. Then they walked into the wagon and took a seat, pretending that they had been there all along. On their way back through the square, they saw a dramatic scene:
–COME OUT OF THERE, Party Secretary Rana was shouting through a bullhorn at a bunch of men barricaded on the first floor of the Bruckenthal Museum, AND WE WILL SETTLE EVERYTHING PEACEFULLY!

A man, leaning out the museum window, held the gallery's most precious painting, *Ignazio de Loyola* by Rubens, at arm's length, and shouted back:

–IF WE CAN'T HAVE THE CEMETERY YOU CAN'T HAVE THIS! He poked a finger through Ignazio's face.

At this juncture, the tramway moved out of sight, and all Andrei's later efforts to find out what had happened were in vain. He often, in later years, would go to the Bruckenthal Museum and stare intently at Ignazio's face. There seemed to be not a trace of a finger there. Had he dreamt the whole thing? Or was it Francis Xavier that the man had poked?

As he walked home, unconsciously jingling the gold in his pocket, he reviewed the events of the day. It was the sight of his hard-on, leading him into the Oval that preoccupied him the most. He had the distinct feeling that his cock was some kind of divining rod pointing (when it got hard) toward some precise event in the future.

It began to rain.

Soon, Mother and Purgu would return. It was the end of summer, the end of something. He was ready for the lycée, the awesome school he had been told "separates the cream from the ashes."

BOOK TWO

10

"Childhood is over," said God, looking at him through his mother's eyes, through the eyes of a building he passed on his way home and through an eye in the sky.

"The hell it is," said the Devil. "For the sake of prose, some eyes must be mercifully removed."

Remove then the eye which sees that childhood is over. This eye pans slowly across four years and sees a blue uniform hanging loosely on a skinny body, the concrete walls of the schoolyard in which he paces back and forth with bombs in his head, the endless streams of worthless facts and phenomena they are stuffing into his brain, a suspicious gas they make him drink . . . behind these externals, in the background, the eye picks up youth organizations, terrified teachers lighting little candles under the icon of Marx, Party people, partly people, and so on. And if it's a particularly sharp eye, it will also detect, behind all of this, the vague shape of History, an entity without friends or enemies, sitting unmoved at the top of an abstract cliff. Having seen all this, the eye sees the razor blade . . . what a mess.

–I may be eighty-two years old, *Mon vieux*, but I can spot talent where I see it . . . this child is a genius. . . .

–Let us not hasten to make such statements, dear comrade . . . He is a defiant element. Having said this, the UTC (Union of Communist Youth) Secretary slicked back the two hairs on his otherwise bald head, smoothed his leather jacket, and excused himself. He walked into the meeting hall.

83

The meeting hall was, as always, packed. The uniformed students stood up and began singing the "International."

The eighty-two-year-old man, who was the town's most famous writer (he had written 125 historical novels and 16 romances) looked after the Secretary with disgust. He was an aristocrat, he definitely hated this new breed of leather-jacketed political commissar with "chicken brains" as he kindly called them. He turned to leave the school's chancellery when he caught sight of a pale and erect Ivanovitch who had, apparently, overheard the elusive dialogue.

—Now don't let that go to your head, the old man said. I intervened for you so that you can keep publishing . . . but, please *mon cher*, get on with school . . . If they expel you there is nothing anyone can do. . . .

Ivanovitch walked into the meeting. He was, as usual, late. Everyone turned to look at him.

—This resolution is hereby put to a vote, the Secretary continued, paying him no notice. Yes? All the hands in the room went up. They were all for it.

—Abstaining?

Nobody.

—No?

Nobody.

The resolution, passed in his absence, called for a new meeting at which time Andrei Ivanovitch Goldmutter would confess all his sins. Self-criticism, it was called.

All this was the fault of "The Eagle." He had written a poem called "The Eagle," dedicated to the UTC. *Eminescu, the greatest Rumanian poet, had syphilis. Caragiale, the greatest playwright, was a dropout. All the other greats had run away with the Gypsies, killed themselves, fallen into the river, had been put in jail*, this is what the poem, in brief, had contained. It ended with two ironic lines in which the question was asked: *Does the Union of Communist Youth have a medicine for me? If so, is it bitter or sweet?*

84

In the first place, the Secretary had said, who the hell gave him the right to say he's great? In the second, this Jew has a lot of nerve. And, finally, why are his poems being published in the local paper? Who was behind it? In his search for the person(s) behind it, the Secretary went to the head of the Red Star Workshop, to which Ivanovitch belonged. The head of it was none other than the venerable old master, Dr. Tudor, who had, as just seen, told him off. Next, he went "higher," to the Party Secretariat. He may have gone even higher than that. For everybody "high," there was someone "higher." This going "above" is, in fact, a Rumanian pastime and, in simplified drawings of a Rumanian's life, we see a ladder beginning directly at the top of his head and disappearing into the clouds. No one knew how "high" the Secretary had gone on the matter of "The Eagle," but the day for the "self-criticism" session soon came.

Ivanovitch went completely unprepared. The sin of pride, as it were, did not bother him. He didn't feel there was anything to confess. At first, he had composed a number of arrogant speeches in his defense. But then he spent the day before the UTC meeting in the Bruckenthal Museum in front of miracles, desert saints, virgin births, dark Flemish forests and bishops dressed from head to foot in purple and black velvet with gold chains dangling from their necks and the shiny heads of infant Jesuses sparkling in the middle of those. He felt elected to a special understanding with these images and soon they all came together in his head and formed the word God. God, who was this composite of painterly opulence, guarded him from crude intrusions and allowed him to disregard school entirely. God wasn't alone on the job. Father was also there and Father, like God, possessed a thousand attributes and a thousand images. He was a car racer, a bandit, a painter, a partisan. He wore leathers and he had a gun. When Ivanovitch walked into the UTC meeting hall he had God on his right, Father on his left and between them strode the delicious and recurrent vision of Comrade P, his Russian teacher, who held him, in this vision, after class and then slipped her ringed hand under the belt of his pants and her miniskirt went up as far as her, no doubt, richly endowed pubic mound. He knew, walking in like this, that a tremendous diversion would spare him the pain of talking.

This diversion came in the form of . . . the Kennedy assassination. It so happened that the school had acquired a television set. This set, of which there were one thousand in the whole country, was completely useless because there were no TV stations. The rumor had it, however, that one would be built any day. The machine sat on a little platform in the UTC hall and, at the beginning of every meeting, it was turned on so that the assembled youth could watch test patterns. This ritual was supposed to induce reverence for the technical progress of the Republic. The Secretary, on this particular day, switched on the set and . . . through the previously blank screen, a medley of unbelievable images poured into the room. It was the Assassination, live, and in black-and-white from the U.S.A. via satellite. The confused voice of the first Rumanian TV announcer crackled through the static with the facts: the relay station had been completed and hooked into the satellite a few hours before . . . Kennedy had been assassinated . . . In view of the gravity of the situation, the Party had decided to let every-one watch the news and confusion from the U.S. directly . . . It was a sad event to mark the beginning of Rumanian TV, but . . . he said, the bitter truth does not choose its time. The images they were seeing, he said, would prove, without any doubt, that the capitalist world was collapsing. This was, without any further doubt, proven. Andrei remembers that above and under the numbing shock of the news, he was completely fascinated by the pictures of American cities, cars and people. There were buildings he could not believe existed . . . As many cars on one street as Rumania had citizens . . . Amazing incomprehensible things written in ten meter letters on the walls . . . Through this came a metallic voice in English . . . The confused Rumanian commen-tator translated bits and pieces. It was incredible . . . they were sent home.

His mother was in the kitchen, glued to the radio.
 –Did you hear? she said.
 –I saw, he managed to whisper.

86

—It's a plot, said Mother, a plot by the Russians to start a war
. . . They made the whole thing up. . . .

But the radio was also confirming it. And not the Rumanian radio.
They were listening to "Radio Free Europe" and "The Voice of
America," free of jamming for the first time since 1948.

Mother didn't sleep all night. She turned from one station to the
other, watching the tiny light of the dial crossing the Atlantic.
Strangely, Andrei felt responsible for what happened, as if his
private world had created the catastrophe. Father was dead, Stalin
was dead and, every time, he had somehow forecast the events.
It's not true, he told himself, feeling the source of that power. But
inside he knew: this is what happens to the world if a child makes
up his father over and over.
    —The technological age has come to Rumania with a bang, said
Dr. Tudor the next day . . . The silver hoof is on our foreheads.

They were sitting around the desk of the Red Star Workshop a
few minutes before the scheduled start of the meeting. Ivanovitch
looked around. Almost everyone was there: the old, the young, the
curious, the informers.
    Nister, the lawyer who hadn't pleaded a case in five years,
looked out the window at the brightly lit square with the Party
Headquarters on the center and said:
    —It's like the day Stalin died . . . everybody is crying on the
streets . . . I think Rumanians love funerals . . . It's a chance for
them to let go of all the repressed feelings and tear their hair in
public. . . .
    —So, so, your Honor . . . said Anrad, ironically, I suppose you
don't feel troubled about anything. . . .
    —I am a philosopher . . . The things of this world are of equal
importance to me . . . This is why I am not in court any longer
. . . I want to do *nothing* in great style. . . .
    —How about doing something for the people? asked the Work-
shop Secretary, who was a notorious Stalinist responsible for jail-
ing at least six writers no longer than ten years ago.

87

At this, the little, nervous old men who had been recently freed from jail (on the wake of "liberalization") clutched their tiny notebooks and hummed indistinctly. Their handwriting was as tiny as their notebooks, a habit acquired, no doubt, in jail where they had little paper. One of these men, Lad Anu, showed Andrei a novel he had written on one sheet of typing paper during six years of solitary confinement. It looked wrought by a mad spider. Anu had, during all those years, filled this piece of paper with what he thought was writing but what was, in reality, a solid square of blackness.

It was the beginning of a typical session of the Red Star Workshop. Ideological fights went on late into the night. Six generations of writers came into contact here, their views and fears mingling in bursts of passion. Occasionally, a poem or a story would be read which left no doubt as to its antiregime nature . . . At these times, the Workshop Secretary and his six cronies who were the political watchdogs, began to snarl and attack. It was a heated atmosphere which would, often, continue all night at some bar and there were times when blows followed insults.

The UTC had merely postponed his public confession. Overlooking "crimes" of even smaller magnitudes would not happen. He went to the meeting with the collar of his jacket raised. A great sign of rebellion! The horrible blue uniforms which everyone tried desperately to personalize allowed little play. His personal contribution had been to raise his collar, a gesture which became instant fashion. The gesture was duly noticed and, after the meeting was called to order, the Secretary directed the following at Ivanovitch:
  –Put that collar down!
  –I'm afraid that's not possible, he said, because this collar keeps my head up and without it, it would fall off.

His confession was not needed. Everybody voted YES, yes, they had to expel him for two weeks until he straightened up. His schoolmates! What a bunch of sheep! The world was turning upside down, presidents were gunned down and they agreed in mass to punish him for raising his collar . . . Degrees of irrelevance!

This was fine with him, he could use two weeks of uninterrupted vagabonding . . . but a few days later the matter went "higher."

SECRETARY RANA WANTS TO SEE YOU! he was told, the day he returned to school.

Now, Secretary Rana was a big man. He controlled, mildly put, the destinies of his town. As Secretary General of the Party, his duties included such things as mass executions and delivery of production figures to the Central Committee. That he should concern himself with this kind of matter indicated that there was a great slump in interest, a time, therefore, to direct hostile symbology and other intellectual activities. Comrade Rana did, in fact, read poetry and made careful notes of the things he didn't understand (mostly everything). These notes filled several voluminous dossiers labeled "Dialectic Growth of Symbolic Logic." By "symbolic logic," he did not mean what you and I mean, he simply meant to find out if the symbols expressed by poets, writers and journalists were "logical." This "logic" was the Party Line. Normally, this kind of work is done by a cultural commissar but, as we've said, the Secretary was something of an intellectual and had assimilated the position for which he paid himself an extra salary.

Ivanovitch walked through the baroque door (with his collar neatly raised) and gave his name to the armed guard on the third floor. The upholstered black wall slid sideways and, stepping firmly on the thick red carpet, he advanced toward the Secretary's desk. This desk, in itself a masterpiece of baroque leisure, was supported by winged mahogany creatures.

–Put your collar down, said the Secretary.
–I'm sorry, Comrade Rana, it is not possible.
–Why? said the astonished man touching his carefully shined silver hair.

89

–Because it is an important part of my personality.

–Sit down.

He did.

–What is so special about personality, yours, I mean?

–I am a poet. I am, therefore, different from everybody else.

This, visibly, opened the Secretary's book of Marxist dialectics to page 234 where it says that: "Difference, as espoused by the petty bourgeois artist, is a symptom of the decadence of bourgeois society." This took a moment to assimilate.

–You are, I suppose, at the age of sixteen, proud to be different from the peasant who sweats twenty-four hours in the fields to hasten the building of Socialism?

–Not proud, Comrade, just different.

–Young man, you are arrogant, irrational, uncontrollable, and I could easily throw you out of school . . . this matter is ridiculous . . . (here he paused and frowned) but . . . I have read your poetry in the "Flame" and, I must admit, it is logical. . . .

–Which poem are you referring to, Comrade? (He had published four.)

–The one about . . . er . . . Socialism being like a milk pail emptied into the stomachs of people . . . er . . . while the Cow of Mother Nature is turning red . . . that was some fit of dialectics. . . .

–Thank you, Secretary, he said, obviously impressed.

–Of course, of course, beamed the man, pleased with himself. Tell you what . . . you put that damned collar down and we can talk about poetry every week . . . The futility of it all.

–I am sorry. . . .

–I know, I know, he shouted, it's your personality . . . get out of here!

The matter was over. In his haste to make a victorious exit, he bumped into the guard. When he reached the bottom of the stairs, his jacket collar had grown all around his head like a lettuce and it kept growing until it reached the top of the Party Building and then it began growing downward until it had completely covered six floors. Keeps the cold out, he grinned.

He walked into the Turkish Cafe across from the Lyceum (strictly out of bounds) and sat right in front of the plate glass window with a black Turkish coffee and a cognac in front of him. A cigarette dangled from the corner of his mouth.

11

He climbed on top of the dresser and, looking at the ceramic statue of Napoleon gathering dust there, masturbated furiously. Mother walked in just as the last drop landed on the door.

–Had a hard day at work? he asked.

. . . He wondered if Ina was home . . . Ina was the Gypsy girl downstairs who, about a week ago, had dropped her slip, as if by mistake, and stood there stark naked staring at him. After staring back at her for a long time, he tried to get up but she had already put the thing back on saying, "Still too young. . . ."

She wasn't home. He headed for the cafe.

Itt was already there, reading conspicuously a "Pleiade" edition of Mallarme. Stoica had also arrived. He was resting his head against the back of his chair, listening with his eyes half closed to Dr. Pradu, a gynecologist interested in literary matters, who laced all his speeches with professional metaphors.

Two old maids, in a state of perpetual excitement, passed poems back and forth. Dr. Pradu glanced at them, occasionally, with the worried look of someone who has just discovered a new disease.

–As I was saying, Pradu went on, your generation has nothing to hook in to . . . For twenty years there hasn't been a shred of intelligent writing in this country . . . You read Lucian Blaga, Ion Barbu, Eliade, Baciu, Tzara, Vinea and the rest . . . But to you they are heroes the way a surgical glove is a hero to a man without hands . . . These writers, geniuses as they may be, had a living

92

context for all their writing . . . Take them out of their context and all their prejudices, along with their virtues, become mannerisms. . . .

–What else do you expect us to do? said Itt in an irritable voice. We can't get any foreign books so we have no idea what the hell goes on in other countries . . . we can't even find all of Blaga, Vinea and the rest . . . and here we are stuck with Mihai Beniuc and Nina Cassian, two Socialist pieces of shit.

–Ssshh . . . Ssshhh . . . said Stoica.

–The fact is, said Pradu, that poetry has a certain kind of power in this country . . . All the bureaucrats are intellectuals . . . every single book of poetry is sold out . . . When I go out of the abortion room, no one waits for me to shake my hand . . . when you read a poem, there is always a reaction. . . .

–That's because abortions are useful, said Ivanovitch. Poetry is nothing. I just burned up all my poems. I'm taking up mathematics. . . .

–Ha ha ha, laughed Stoica. Whatever made you do it?

–My sex life.

–Sooner or later you'll all come to me, said Dr. Pradu.

Other cafe regulars came by. Vidrighin, the peasant, who had, since elementary school become a little more sophisticated, and who, by virtue of having been born in the same village as Octavian Goga, the great nationalist poet, assumed an air of native superiority. He hated French poets. Perhaps because he didn't speak a word of French, despite insistent schooling.

Zinga, the pretty Gypsy boy, who comprehended not a word of what was being said, came mainly to let himself be admired by the homosexuals of the cafe who drooled over him.

–This question of homosexuality, Pradu expounded, is very delicate in Rumania . . . Overtly, one could go to jail for five years for sucking boy cock but, in practice, the six hundred years of Turkish occupation have made this act a lot more natural than eating pussy, for example . . . Even so, if they catch you *in flagrante delicto* (he pointed a finger at Ivanovitch), they can send you up for a long time. . . .

93

–Don't worry about me, Pradu. I can hardly suck on my cigarette.

Walking home he thought about poetry. It was truly the only medium people could criticize their government in. This is why it was so popular. But mathematics, ah mathematics, that was something entirely different . . . "you can only know God intellectually through mathematics" (Philip Lamantia) . . . Why, certainly . . . Ion Barbu had been a distinguished mathematician and a great poet . . . Enter the Distinguished Mathematician: "Allow me to pick this little number from your hair . . . It is a piece of the integral I am working on . . . It flew out the window and caught in your hair" . . . Damn. He was thinking of women again.

Even though it was dark and a little cold, he decided to stay on. There was somebody else sitting on a bench. A girl. He tried to not look at her. He had too many infatuations already. What is easier than to fall madly in love with a girl shivering on a park bench in the dark? He was infatuated, by the latest count, with twenty-six women, twelve men, and one mailbox. This mailbox stood on the corner of his street and every time he returned late, it assumed the wistful shape of a beautiful woman pushing her provocative hips forward with a clear intent . . . Who was that girl on the bench, anyway? So close to his house? Perhaps he knows her . . . He got up, sat down again, then, resolutely walked toward the stranger.
    –In the name of Lenin, Stalin and the Communist Party of Rumania, what is your name? he said. She didn't answer. *It* didn't answer. What was it anyway? It was a giant flower in a smashed flower pot.

He did, finally, get laid that summer. It happened at Vidrighin's farm, in a hayloft. The girl was a Gypsy who had approached him one day when he was walking through the village and asked him if he'd ever taken a train. Yes, he said, he'd taken many trains. She wanted to know all about it. So they went to the hayloft, a place that was her favorite hideout, and he told her about trains. She was fourteen, had pigtails and sparkling black eyes. She

94

showed him how to make love to her and the whole time she asked him to tell her about trains so that, after a while, they were rocking along to the rhythm of a train that was, when all is told, a beautiful rhythm.

In any case, Ivanovitch was ready for other pastures. The Lyceum years were over. He appeared in the Class Portrait without a tie and with his collar raised. He had read, with great gaps, everything he could find in French, Hungarian and German in his hometown. He had notebooks filled with poetry. Notebooks filled with equations. He left without regret. There hadn't been a single teacher worth his remembrance with the exception of Comrade P., to whom he is forever grateful for letting him fuck her between her beautiful, firm, albeit imaginary Greek breasts. To the cafe crowd he said goodbye by buying six bottles of cognac out of his first big check from *Gazeta Literara* (Literary Gazette). To one of the old maids who offered herself to him on the eve of his departure, he says "thank you" again. He is sorry he was too drunk to do it. Au revoir, Cher Maitre Tudor! To Mother who had, meanwhile, divorced the chemical engineer, he said "good luck" with the new lover, an air force pilot.

On the train to Bucharest, he pondered Big Questions. Poetry, he thought, is the art of being kidnapped by circumstances. He was going to enroll in the Mathematics Department of the University of Bucharest. He was full of expectations. The great capital was ahead. Was it ready for him? He was certainly ready for it, and stroking his thin and not-growing-fast-enough moustache, he stretched himself full length on the seat of the empty train compartment and admired himself in the ceiling mirror.

95

12

Bucharest, you are an exciting town, a thrilling metropolis! It is obvious that you love your Jews and your Gypsies! In spite of the fact that Rumanian poetry is in a sorry state and a young man from the provinces has come to rescue it!

In spite of those big new buildings which look imported from the Soviet Union! In spite of everything, your sidewalk cafes revel in an Oriental abandon, your summer gardens tremble with Gypsy violins, the cider is fresh, and your hot sausages turn on grills, incessantly . . . the exuberance of your natives is contagious and here, here is a serious young man about to burst on the literary scene with his boots on as a vast and refreshing wave of barbarism pours out of him. . . .

He felt subversive, exhilarated, determined, intense, amazing, brilliant . . . as he bumped into people, mumbling his excuses, not seeing anyone . . . passionately making love to all the beautiful girls with copies of *Who's Afraid of Virginia Woolf?* in English in their white hands, to the mysterious *femmes fatales* sipping sodas in luxurious restaurants . . . He walked by Capsa, the famous literary cafe since the nineteenth century . . . he introduced himself to a score of the illustrious dead and the fabulous living . . . "Time is of no consequence, old fellow," he said to N. D. Cocea . . . It was fall, the entrance exams to the Mute World of Mathematics were imminent. Although not very well prepared, he felt deep reserves of charm which, as he knew, would override any test.

And, in truth, they did. He sailed breezily through the History of Mathematics, enveloped the orals in a cabbalistic fog and did an excellent job of the "Theorem of the Hypothetical Duck," which was his chosen theme.

Stoica, Itt, and Anrad, who had all entered the Faculty of Letters, fought with the "Hunting Scenes in Nineteenth-century Rumanian Literature" . . . They had all rented a room together, at an outrageous price, from an old hag. When the five exhausting days were over, the confident young musketeers set about town. The results would be announced the following day, a Tuesday.

Between them, they had enough money for a solid week of drinking because the combined sums were their living allowances for one month. They began in the neighborhood of their room but the rather quiet taverns did not measure up to their appetites, so soon they were in the elegant center of town. A few bars, particularly, attracted them. These were especially built for foreign tourists and featured such exotic things as Coca-Cola.

They must have hit the 222nd tavern of the night. Anrad had lost one shoe, Itt had to be carried, Stoica was trying to romantically lure a ninety-year-old whore sitting in an outdoor garden (he couldn't see very well) and Ivanovitch was making speeches.
  –Listen to me, all you carnivorous, hell-bound idiots! Whoever it was that told you about curves becoming circles, lied, and the lie, er, becomes, burp, a lot more trivial when one, er, looks, burp, at Communism, this terrific, er, burp, idea, burp, moving to the beat of a great human, burp sweat puddle . . . I had no father, burp, and no one here did . . . where is the gold?
  The electrified audience vanished as soon as his speech became political. He didn't want them to leave. He would have liked to talk about flowers. But he didn't know the language. Their group, he noticed, had become twice as large. The ninety-year-old whore whom Stoica had managed to pick up was actually young and beautiful. (Perhaps it was *he* who needed the glasses.) They were all sitting on the sidewalk in front of the tavern they had just been thrown out of. Itt had passed out. A tall man with glasses, sitting

97

next to him, complained about his wife and his job which consisted in violently thrashing plastic bags on an assembly line. Stockings? On his other side, a pretty girl with short black hair and a white silk blouse through which her nipples thrust, was holding his hand.

–What is your name? he asked.

–Kira.

–Where did you come from, Kira Kiralina?

–From the Danube. You were a mess so I thought I would take care of you until you stopped talking. Interesting speech too. I saw you at the university today. I was taking my exam by the window on your left . . . She was a nonstop talker.

–Yes, he said, I remember.

–You don't but that's all right . . . I'm not sure it was you.

They all ended up in their rented room on Barzelor Street, tiptoeing through the dark hall so they wouldn't wake up the "tzatza." Tzatza had a ferocious temper. The room had two beds in it and Andrei, holding Kira by the waist, cornered the one by the window where he had slept last night with Itt. The window was open and Kira, kneeling on the bed, stuck her head out of it. The warm but breezy night came in. He cupped her breasts and, glueing himself to her back, he looked out to see what she was seeing.

–I am a virgin, she said.

They were being drawn tighter and tighter toward each other, with their heads still in the dark window, and he began to sober up as every fine hair on his body stood up. She turned around, facing him abruptly, and said:

–I'm thirsty.

They made love. Flashes of sheet lightning illuminated the room. Much later, he caught a brief glimpse of the others, locked in a surrealist tableau on the floor: the ninety-year-old whore who had, again, turned ninety, was twisted like a reptilian cloud holding both Stoica and Anrad in a two-headed embrace. Itt was asleep, spread on the other bed like a broken umbrella. The tall man with glasses stood facing the mirror, naked, holding his cock and murmuring: "Wait till my wife hears about this." Then there was a burst of thunder and it started to rain.

His headache, next day, was serious but he felt light, free and exhilarated. It was eleven o'clock. By God, he thought, surveying the room, they've announced the results. This thought woke everybody up. The man with glasses had vanished. Kira gave a start and hastily began putting on her clothes. Itt woke violently hitting the wall with his head. Stoica and the beautiful thin girl who now stood in place of last night's old whore, rose together off the floor in one movement. On the way out, his clothes a mess, Andrei surveyed the ravaged room.

They had all passed. Itt, Anrad, Stoica, Kira and Ivanovitch linked arms and danced on the street. They were all Comrade students now! In the big, marvelous town! The rain had washed the side-walks clean.

13

"There was a time," he wrote in an introduction to a group of his poems published in *Luceafarul, "when my imagination served me mainly to get through the Lyceum. I used to walk through my classroom walls into another, imaginary classroom, filled with the girls I liked. I was playing the fool, naturally. I also loved to torture the one-legged school principal who walked through the yard looking for his missing limb which I had hidden in the attic. The principal climbed all the stairs (with great difficulty) but just as he reached the attic, I would let the leg fall again all the way to the first floor. The man hobbled downstairs only to have the trick played on him, with infinite patience, until the end of time when the deformed Sisyphuses of the world shall be released."*

"I have not," he continued, *"given up on this use of my imagination. Only the subject matter has changed. The questions before me, today, are these: WHY ARE WE BEING DEPRIVED OF OUR PAST? WHERE ARE THE CLASSICS OF OUR POETRY? WHY HAS THERE BEEN NO REPRINTING OF BOOKS BY BLAGA, VINEA, FUNDOIANU, TZARA, ELIADE, MATEI CARAGIALE AND MANY MORE? WHY ARE THERE MORE CRITICS THAN POETS? WHAT IS SOCIALIST REALISM? WHAT IS THE HEROIC STURDINESS OF SQUARE-JAWED LARGER-THANLIFESIZE WORKERS POURING STEEL INTO APOCALYPTIC VATS? WHERE ARE THE TRANSLATIONS? WHY HAVE THE LIBERTIES BEEN ALWAYS GRANTED FROM THE TOP? WHY HAVE THE RUSSIAN*

*POETS, IN MANY WAYS NOT AS INTERESTING AS
OURS, INFLUENCED THEIR SOCIETY SO MUCH
MORE THAN OURS HAVE? WHY CAN'T WE GO
STUDY ABROAD, JOIN INTERNATIONAL CONFER-
ENCES AND TRAVEL FREELY? So, you can see the mode
of my imagination has not changed. Instead of torturing my school
principal, I am now torturing myself with the same kind of cruel
and, no doubt, unsolvable type of riddle.*

This was a dangerous piece of literature. It made quite a stir
at the Faculty of Letters.

Kira, whom he saw again because "as it happened," they had a
French class in common, listened patiently to all his fantasies. She
was beautiful. She would throw her short-cut reddish-black hair
over her shoulder, with a nervous gesture, and smile mysteriously.
She was from western Transylvania, a part of the country known
for its beautiful women. Sitting in the cafe, her chair pulled
slightly away from the table, she stretched her legs and leaned
toward him, intently. She disagreed fiercely with what he had just
said and her face had become a diamond. Her eyebrows curled
down and her lips curled up. Her room at the dormitory had the
same shape. She hung pictures on the wall obliquely and had even
arranged her bed to meet the wall at an angle. She wore blouses
with diamond shaped patterns on them and, generally, behaved
toward the world as if all things came in at an angle. In
Hunedoara, where she had lived alone with her mother, the
obliqueness of life had come upon her early. Her mother's eyebrows, she once told him, went up while hers went down. Her
mother's lips were always curling down because men were always
leaving her. Kira tried to smile. Andrei found, talking to her, that
she took very little for granted. He had to always prove what had
before seemed obvious. This quality of hers both unnerved and
enchanted him.

One time, while they were walking past various exhibits in the
Anthropology Museum, they noticed that no one was around.
Hiding behind a dimly lit and enormous display of the "earliest
man in Rumania," they began kissing. In no time at all, they were
making love standing up. They began doing it all over the place

101

but mostly in Cismigiu Park which had marvelous big bushes and they also spared no quiet place anywhere else: bathrooms, ruins, empty classrooms, museums. The sparsely populated small museums were pure heaven. It was so good that ever since, he could not walk into a museum without getting an erection. In his room, which was still occupied by Itt, Stoica and Anrad, they couldn't go. Tzatza had seen them once and nearly thrown them out. Housing was scarce. But he was thinking constantly of Kira. When he didn't see her for a day, he became nervous, irritable, and terribly jealous. She lived in a dormitory in the new part of town but an old tramway made the trip in fifteen minutes. In the hallways, at school, they were inseparable.

She began to write. She wrote a "hypnosis" story followed by another "hypnosis" story and then by another. In every one of these, the subject was hypnotized before the story began and, because of this terrible state, he or she began making political points. The hypnotized girl would roll her eyes backward and proceed to tell about her life in a Soviet concentration camp, for instance. These stories, to his knowledge, were never published. But they circulated. Kira had heard a lot about her subjects in the town she was from.

The editorial offices of many of the literary reviews were a combination of cafe, salon and workshop. Poets met critics here, novelists met each other and, when there was no political commissar around, the talk was free. The thirst for information was fantastic. Foreign plays, poets and events were discussed for hours. The lucky few who could travel abroad brought back books and records. It is here where he got his first glimpses of American poetry. The "Beats" were fairly well known. Typewritten translations (mostly atrocious) made the rounds. The many discussions, of course, revolved around French poetry, which everybody read in the original. All of this found, unfortunately, no echoes in the pages of the reviews themselves. Faint references, yes. But, for the most part, tractors, peasants, Party Secretary quotes and other socialist paraphernalia filled the pages.

102

Kira and he walked the streets all night, improvising poetry and getting drunk. After a particularly stirring night, he wrote a long poem called "Trains." This was a tender and angry ballad about the trains in his life, his sexual experiences on them ("To fuck to the rhythm of trains/Which is the rhythm of Rumania"), about what he imagined to be the life of all the people traveling on trains, including that of convicts being taken to labor camps in cattle wagons. The poem ended with an appeal to his "dead father who had blown up trains" to come ride with him on this new train of life in his country and to see if it was worth it because if it wasn't he too would blow it up and join his old man.

As soon as he had typed this thing up, he called Itt, Stoica and Anrad out of their holes. Kira was already there. They went to a cafe. He read it to them. There was a thick silence.
  –You'll never get away with it, said Stoica.
  –Why not?
  –It's fabulous, said Itt.
  –It needs work, said Anrad.
  –It's the best thing you've ever done, said Kira.
  –It's no good, said Stoica.
  –Why not?
  –It's not a Rumanian poem.
  They hadn't had a fight over this for a long time. Stoica had been changing. He had always been a bit of a nationalist but, lately, he had revised his stands on all kinds of things. ("It is obvious," went one of his sayings, "that Jews, after such exhausting wandering, have lost their direction. Their God has become Gold and their mother has become REHTOM, which sounds like 'rectum' but is really 'mother' upside down.")
  –What's Rumanian? said Kira.
  –Perhaps I should change my name too, suggested Ivanovitch, ironically.
  –I think you should, said Stoica. Who wants to read poetry by Andrei Ivanovitch Goldmutter?
  --Fuck you, Stoica, said Kira, who became salty when angry. Itt laughed.

103

Goldmutter climbed on the table. He was a little drunk and he did something which he would hear, in a funny way, ten years later on the Lower East Side of New York, when Allen Ginsberg said something similar though in a different context.

He shouted as loud as he could:

–My name is Andrei Ivanovitch Goldmutter! Andrei Ivanovitch was bestowed upon me by my dear mother who thought a Russian name would save me from being shot by our friends from the Soviet Union.

–Shut up, said Kira, worried. The cafe was full of students.

But he didn't care.

–Goldmutter is a grand old Jewish name meaning *goldmother* which is what Jews are known for being obsessed with.

The scene was turning ugly. Several people were leaving. The general drunk atmosphere of the cafe had become oppressively silent.

–Shut up, said Stoica. He too was getting worried.

–My friends here, he continued, are of the opinion that I should give up these great natural advantages (he was very loud now) and take on a good Rumanian name so that when my books are in every household, your average Rumanian sonofabitch could look at the name and say ISN'T OUR NATION GREAT AND AREN'T FOREIGNERS DISGUSTING?

Anrad tried to pull him off the table. He pushed Anrad away.

–And I think they are right. So in honor of this great moment which you are witnessing, I would like everyone here to put forward a suggestion regarding my new name.

–Well, you can keep Andrei, shouted a drunk from the back of the room, that's as Rumanian as they come. My father's name was Andrei and he was like an empty wine bottle from the Danube.

The silence was now absolute.

–One down, he said. We will keep Andrei. Now what do we do with Ivanovitch?

–Fuck Ivanovitch, said the drunk. Drop that one altogether.

–Dropped. And now we come to the big one. What do we stick inside Goldmutter to make it uncircumcised again?

The drunk said nothing and since he had been the only one talking, the silence deepened considerably.

–Well, he said, I have no choice but to name myself. Let's see, how about BASTARD? he said, remembering Cobza, his Phys. Ed. teacher.

–Nah, said the drunk.

–Well, how about something like PULALUNGA (Long Prick)?

–Nah, said Anrad, who was warming up.

–Then how about CURVESCU (sonofabitch)?

–That's a thought, said the drunk, but I think you should be a sonofabitch from the woods because you got dark hair.

–Codruvrescu.

–Codrescu, said the drunk.

–Andrei Codrescu.

He got off the table, poured the remaining wine in the drunk's empty glass and got out, leaving them all standing in the thick quiet.

Kira ran after him.

–Andrei Ivanovitch, she said.

–Andrei Codrescu, he corrected her and they walked arm in arm to her dormitory and said good night.

14

If only this side of the story is told, one might get the impression that he was feeling extremely self-important. This wasn't the case. Actually, he felt stupid. "It is possible," he thought, "to be a genius and be completely stupid at the same time."

He had already forgiven Stoica for provoking the scene at the cafe. But Itt and Kira had not. Anrad was ambiguous. Stoica had been one of his best friends throughout Lyceum days but, as between friends, he often hated him. He hated his big, square head full of stringy red hair and, most of all, he hated Stoica's servility. This peasant streak was to be overlooked most of the time, but Stoica was using this native trait to get ahead . . . his servility turned into arrogance as soon as his interests had been served. Stoica moved out. This was a relief.

For the next few days, with Kira, he made the tour of editorial offices, trying to get "Trains" published. The response was identical:

–We publish this, said the bright new young editor of *Gazeta Literara*, and I will soon have a new job. . . .

–Take this thing to America, another said. There nobody cares.

They made sixteen copies of the poem and passed them around.

A few months passed.

One day, Stoica, who had completely disappeared, accosted him on the street and took his arm.

–Did you hear? he said

–Hear what?

106

–I've been put in charge of the political section of UTC at Letters. Isn't that a great joke?

–Yeah. A real joke.

–There have been some rumors . . . (he stopped significantly; he already had the manners of a Communist bureaucrat) . . . they say you have been passing around some anti-Communist propaganda. . . .

–You mean "Trains"? You can't be serious . . . You were there when I first read it. . . .

–I don't know *what* you've been passing around but . . . If I were you, I'd be more careful.

–You're not me, sweetheart, so don't worry.

As Kira and he kept growing closer, Anrad and Itt decided, out of a sense of friendship, to move out and leave them the room. This was such an unexpected gift; they cried and kissed their friends. There was only a little obstacle. Tzatza would not hear of it unless they were married. They decided to get married.

His mother arrived from Sibiu and Kira's mother came from Hunedoara. It was an unpleasant meeting. His mother obviously considered herself vastly superior to the other woman (She had, after all, been married to an *engineer.*) . . . The other woman could not stand the idea that her daughter was marrying a Jew. She was only a worker in a textile mill, but, at least, she was pure *Rumanian.*

The wedding was performed by a disgusted civil servant at the courthouse. He, naturally, didn't like it either. What his reasons were, however, is a blessed mystery. After the wedding they went to a little restaurant where everyone sat around uncomfortably twisting their wine glasses in their hands until his mother looked at her watch and said:

–I have to catch the train in twenty minutes . . . O, my God, where is my mind?

The other woman, who had no watch, was also suddenly reminded:

–Me too. My train leaves too.

They kissed perfunctorily. Good riddance!

107

She was his wife. And his wife was pregnant. The street had done it. Berzelor Street means Street of the Storks. They should have known. Student Aid, which is what they lived on, meant food, occasionally, a lot of wine and a lot of back rent which they endlessly promised to Tzatza, who had, since their marriage, become very friendly. But keeping the baby was out of the question. He felt bad for not being rich. He had a dream in which he found himself in a room full of drawers. The room had no ceiling and the drawers went up into the sky. He kept opening them furiously. They were all empty. "Where the hell did you put the baby?" he shouted, and woke up. Kira smiled sweetly. She was sad.

–There are enormous battles, she said, in the spirit world, between spirits. The spirits fight between themselves for incarnation. The winning spirit finds a womb and settles down waiting to get born.

In March she went to an abortion clinic, payed thirty leis, walked in. It was all free, legal, unproblematic. Twenty minutes later she came out. She was pale. They walked quietly home. A late March snow fell.

Spring came, soon enough. They regained their natural joviality. A review in Cluj accepted "Trains" for publication. This review was testing the air with his poem. Triumphantly, he showed the magazine to whoever cared to look. Now he had two dangerous public statements to his credit. His "Introduction" and "Trains." He was preparing the third. Seeing Stoica in the hall one day, he thrust the magazine under his nose.

–See, he said, they've published it under my new name: Andrei Codrescu.

Stoica was pale.

–You are crazy, you know that . . . Those crazy fools are testing with your poem . . . You could be expelled for this kind of thing and God knows what else. . . .

–I thought they told you in the Party not to say "God."

108

—If you don't want to listen to me, who will you listen to? I am a poet too and your only protector if anything happens . . . The UTC Secretary has already shown the dean at Mathematics a typewritten copy of this thing. . . .

—Yes, but now it's *published!*

Stoica didn't argue with that.

A curious phenomenon was going on. Power was, mysteriously, bestowed upon his friends. Itt, who was as gentle as a lamb and about as political as one, was made director of the student radio station, "The Voice of Youth," another powerful political post.

—It's a new virus, he said to Itt when next he saw him.

Itt was embarrassed.

—It wasn't really my fault, you know. Someone up there (he pointed up) is looking after me.

—Next thing you know, you and Stoica will be in the Central Committee.

—Fat chance, laughed Itt.

But, since it can now be told, this came to pass. Those two are today, if not in the Central Committee, then very close to it.

Anrad, the only one who had neither the taste nor the solid social background required for those positions, kept writing his poetry and thinking about a novel.

—The Ascension is an elevator, said Kira, paraphrasing Dali, which moves up because of the weight of the dead body of Christ.

Then it was Kira's turn to get into trouble.

She was "given the opportunity" as Vrancea, the Party Secretary put it, to denounce the "decadent new poetry" that some students were writing, in an article for the Party paper. Secretary Vrancea was perfectly aware that Kira was his wife and, somewhere in his spidery bureaucratic brain, the idea had taken root that he would show everybody, without touching him, that no one believed in this "decadent poetry." Now, it must have taken a very stupid man to think that Kira would do anything like that.

109

She flatly told him what she thought of the idea, and used, in the process, some of the most colorful language she could summon. Well, this was Secretary Vrancea of the *Communist* Party and not some UTC Secretary. The man was boiling in his own juices. He went to see the Dean of Mathematics. The dean, a brilliant mathematician and a gentleman, didn't even listen to the whole thing.

–As far as I am concerned, he said, he is an excellent student and I see no reason for expelling him. He wasn't an "excellent" student but the dean had, no doubt, his own reasons for snubbing the Secretary. But, as always, he found his man.

Dr. Serpea (Snake), an assistant at Philosophy, wrote Vrancea's article to order. The article appeared in *Scineia* (the official Party organ). *"A radical conspiracy within the University,"* went this piece of journalism, *"is trying to import foreign goods into our tradition in order to foster discontent and destroy the healthy foundations of Socialist Realism."* This was very strong language. It was rarely heard in Rumania and, since Khrushchev, it hadn't been heard in the Soviet Union.

He became *persona non grata* at the offices of the literary reviews. All the poets, with the exception, of course, of Itt and Anrad, shunned them. Everyone was expecting the worst.

–You've killed it for all of us, said Stoica.

–You just keep eating shit, said Kira, and you'll be all right. This little conversation topped it all.

An emergency session of the UTC was called. They were both invited, naturally, but he didn't go. Kira went alone because she wanted to fight it. By a resolution of 323 votes FOR and 1 AGAINST (Kira's) he was expelled from the university. Kira came back in tears.

–It was a mockery, she said. Vrancea read for an hour from a phony "complaint" about you and he quoted, all out of context, from "Trains," and said that your father was a traitor to the

Revolution and you are following his footsteps . . . Stoica didn't say a word. He voted FOR. . . .

    —Well, at least they left you alone.

    —I stood up and tried to talk but I was crying and before I could wipe my face, they put the resolution to a vote and I was left standing there screaming. . . .

That was that.

15

He wrote a statement which was disguised neither as an "Introduction" nor as a "poem." It was a straightforward manifesto. *"The new tolerance,"* he said, *"applies mostly to modernistic, technically intriguing writing. No serious, realistic works about life in Rumania are being published. Does the Party, perhaps, feel secure enough to allow obscure language, pretentious symbols and complicated images? Of course it does. No one in his or her right mind (except the critics) would plow through tons of verse only to find out that the poet (just like the reader) feels enormously frustrated by almost everything. A good, straight wave of realistic prose would give the people a chance to have a viable, as they say, language."*

He was laughed at by every editor.

–You are an avant-garde writer, said Paunescu. You are following the typical path of the intellectual Jew in this country . . . Soon you will leave and found a neo-Dadaism like Tzara. . . .

According to this theory, modern art was the invention of provincial Rumanian Jews like Tristan Tzara, Isidore Isou and Ilarie Voronca. It wasn't a bad theory but it didn't apply to him. He *was* involved with his country. He had things to do here.

Before the winter was over the two of them took a Christmas vacation at Kira's grandparents, who lived in a little village in western Transylvania.

16

The old folks lived in a peaceful mountain village to which they traveled on slow trains climbing with difficulty over precarious bridges arched in the air on deep gorges at the bottom of which little ice-bound rivers flowed. The walls of these chasms were covered with snow. Kira and Andrei passed the time in the train restaurant. They were the only ones in there. They had endless cups of coffee. Kira reminisced about the region where she had spent her early childhood. She remembered stories of people eaten by wolves in winter, of ice and snow fairies who lived in every crevice, of wrinkled old ladies made of black snow who lived at the mouth of the Life and Death Springs. The Life Spring (which is always the goal of the fairy-tale hero because he has to bring some back to revive the dead princess) is at the very top of the tallest mountain and can be reached only after great trials and dangers. And even if one gets there, it is easy to mistake the Life Spring with the Death Spring and return with the wrong water. One must have very good guides to pick the right stuff. One hero never made it, even though he had Saint Monday, Saint Tuesday, Saint Wednesday, Saint Thursday, Saint Saturday and Saint Sunday on his side. He had inadvertently slighted Saint Friday. Kira also told him a vampire story, the only one he had ever heard in Transylvania proper. Well, here it is, and may it set the rumors to rest.

A very rich man, who, before he died, ate gold every day, hoping in this way to take his vast fortune to the grave, went to see a Sage. "I could never eat all my gold," he bitterly complained, "and I will die soon." "There is a way," said the Sage, "to live forever." "I will give you all my gold," said the rich man, "if you will show me how to do that." The Sage passed his hand over the man's eyes and showed him the place in Heaven where his parents lived. They seemed happy. "Go up to them," said the Sage, "and ask them for their blood." The rich man did just that, and his parents, smiling sadly to see him so unfeeling, opened their necks and all their blood collected in two pools at his feet. "Drink it," said the Sage. Gulp, gulp. The rich man stood up. The Sage then took him to visit all his dead relatives in Heaven, Hell and Purgatory and, from all of them, he asked for blood. After he was as full as he could be, the Sage told him to go away because he had gained immortality. The only way, however, to maintain this state was to constantly drink living people's blood and never quench his thirst until he found blood tasting like that of his mother. This was, obviously, impossible, because until the end of time he would always be among the living and his mother would always be among the dead.

So there!

Kira's grandparents met them at the station in a small troika pulled by a grey mare. They extricated themselves from the crowd of peasants getting off the train with their city purchases and whole fences of rolled up wire on their backs, and got inside the thing which began to roll smoothly over the snow.

A pig had been slaughtered in their honor (traditionally, they only killed one pig every two years because they were poor, the Collective paid them little and, anyway, one pig was plenty for two old folks) so the little wooden house (two small dark rooms) was filled with fresh sausages, liver pastes, fresh hams, bacon, smoked feet and millions of other goodies that a pig provides. The old man slept on the earth oven because it was the warmest place in the house and he had rheumatism and was nearly blind, while his wife occupied a large cloth sack filled with hay and stretched next to the center table under the icon of the Virgin lit up by burning pork fat.

114

They made Kira sleep with her grandmother while Andrei got to curl inside a trunk filled with chicken feathers out of which his legs stuck from the knees down, almost touching the old man on the oven. He did, in fact, that first night, kick him in the face when he turned over, but he hadn't woken up.

Next day they went to church. They were both very happy. The snow, the beautifully dressed peasants in their riots of colors in costumes extinct everywhere else, the little wooden church at the top of a steep hill pointing straight into the cold blue sky, the mountains all around them, the cobbled little street, the terrific smells of food and holiday breads, baking and singing . . . all this . . . What did Communism and all that abstract babbling have to do with all this?

They kneeled in the little church alongside everyone while the bearded priest shook the incense over their heads and the strange litanies of the Orthodox Mass flowed over them and into them and out of them. He was feeling a good, honest emotion. After some fifteen minutes on the cold floor, however, some of it began to dissipate. He felt strange, not really "belonging." He sneaked a look at Kira. There she is, he thought, lost in the religion of her parents. It took her only a second to become one with it . . . But he was wrong. Kira looked back at him and lifted her eyes to the ceiling, meaning clearly, "hope it's over soon." But he was sad yet. He would have liked her to be as absorbed in the service as he couldn't be himself. But as he looked at her again, and saw how beautiful she looked among all the peasants, between the tall candles, he felt a wave of affection. They were so different from these people. Or were they? Or, at least, he was. Was he? Words like "simple clean faith," "unbroken tradition," "mythical space," "mioritic space," echoed through his head. Were they true? The thought, contiguous, that all these people were grouped together in a unit called a "Socialist Collective Commune" just didn't, somehow, make sense. Their collectivity was religious. What other kind of "socialism" would isolated mountain people share? This other outward Collective was only an economic unit for optimum taxation by the State. But since Rumanian peasants

115

have always been taxed ad optimum and ad nauseam, they handled their new situation with grace and with a greater adhesion to their mythical, symbolic collectivism. But this, naturally, applied only to the old folks. The young ones had left or were leaving for the cities and for the construction sites such as the Arges Dam. The village culture was dying.

The following days were an unbroken food and wine orgy. The old timers had a rousing time of it, playing pipes and flutes all day and all night and singing long epic ballads that, at times, lasted long after the fires had gone out and most folks to sleep. They even got to make love the last night because they figured correctly that the old ones would be sleeping like logs after what they'd been through. The trunk was uncomfortable but the chicken feathers were soft and they did it intensely, fast, with passionate precision. In the morning, he had the feeling, as he was waking up, that she was still there and he stroked her tenderly marveling at her softness. When he became fully conscious he saw that he was holding an enormous striped cat staring at him through big green eyes.

On the way back, they spoke little. They let the train rock them. More and more, their life in Bucharest, with all its literary gossip, pompous cafe talk, seemed like a joke. It was a cardboard figure. Working for the *Red Star* was like pissing off a cliff. And Kira, at the university, whiled away her time learning cynicism. The name of the village they had just left was *Apusul de Jos* (The Lower Sunset) and, in some way, the name held a ferocious significance.

17

Everything in Itt's new office, with the exception of the sign on the door which said: VOICE OF YOUTH, RADIO STATION, had been put in through a series of awesome "connections." The new, fluffy rug on the floor came through a Collective President whose commune had been favorably mentioned. The huge, round mirror came from the house of an old bourgeois grocer who had died without heirs. The desk, made of solid brown walnut, had belonged to the office of a Regional Secretary who had just been promoted to the Capital thanks to a few well placed words on the radio. Alexandra, Itt's new secretary, also came from the Regional office. Itt himself, since becoming king of the air, seemed to have just landed on the planet through the machinations of a Sky Bureau. Andrei and Alexandra became friends. She typed up his poems and told him everything she heard in the office. She heard a lot and one of the things she heard was very disturbing. She said that Stoica had been to see Itt a few days before and, it seems, he had told Itt that the armed services were taking a big interest in Codrescu because he wasn't a student any more and his deferment was canceled.

He didn't think the threat was very serious. He knew of another, very famous, Rumanian poet who had talked his way out of the army by reciting Octavian Goga's poetry all night to an astonished Sergeant. He didn't tell Kira.

Not having to go to school any longer, he divided his time between the Academy Library, where he looked up old chronicles and mostly forbidden books, and Itt's office where he wrote inane little articles for pocket money and stared at Alexandra who was tall, had curly black hair, wore purple lipstick and filed her fingernails patiently in search of an elusive perfect roundness. He tried to imagine what it was like to have breasts. At night, he cupped Kira's breasts in his hands and tried, again, to imagine what that would feel like. He was becoming quite obsessed with breasts and one time, as he sat by the window of their room, the sun fell in at a strange angle and he saw, reflected in the glass, his breasts. They were firm, round and jutted away from his chest like startled grapefruits. Kira and Alexandra liked each other and, often, the three of them would go to the movies. Sitting between them he imagined himself to be a four-breasted creature with Kira's eyes and Alexandra's lips. Sometimes it was Alexandra's eyes and Kira's lips. He felt as if he was drawing a magical feminine circle around himself. Outside this circle, the Socialist Republic with its brutal armies, bared its rotten teeth and got closer.

One day, Kira, Andrei and Alexandra were sitting quietly on the fluffy rug in Itt's office, holding hands for some reason, when Itt walked in accompanied by Stoica. The two of them shined in their state-issue nylon windbreakers and they both had their hands in their pockets.

–Oh! said Itt, not a little astonished at what he saw. Stoica lashed out immediately. Addressing Codrescu in a voice which sounded like a beer can rolling on a cement floor, he said:

–You still think that a poet is the maximum irresponsibility a man can pack . . . That decadent stuff went out with Baudelaire.

–What are you talking about? said Kira.

–These kids are too much! shrieked Stoica.

–How old is this guy? said Kira to Itt. He seems young but he acts like an ancient reptile!

Meanwhile, Alexandra calmly got up from the floor, took her seat at the typewriter and began polishing her fingernails looking at Stoica with an amused air.

–You are all decadent foreigners, said Stoica. I bet you smoke

118

hashish. I wouldn't be surprised to see you in a place I won't mention. . . .

–Is that a threat? asked Andrei.

–No, Itt hastened to explain, all he means is that you should watch yourselves because not everybody likes you the way we do. Andrei got up and, for a moment, the possibility of punching Stoica in the face made him dizzy. He was relieved of this possibility when Stoica left abruptly, banging the door.

–Now what have you done? said Itt. And what are you staring at? he shouted ferociously at Alexandra who looked at him from way above the world.

Poor Itt! He liked everybody. It was impossible for him, however, to keep liking everybody in his position.

–Would you mind explaining, said Kira, what got that punk so worked up?

–He seemed to think . . . that the three of you . . . you know . . . it did look rather strange. . . .

–And what business is it of his? shouted Kira. She blushed.

–Well . . . he's just been made UTC Secretary for the whole district . . . everything is his business. . . .

After this incident, Andrei conceived the following simple idea: if it was that man's business to be an informer, it was Codrescu's business to put him on the wrong track. If power was the game, Codrescu was against power. If power, brutality, the army and the Party represented reality then he was against reality. He decided to disguise himself, disappear, fight dirty, be insidious, change identities.

Nothing else was said and when they got home he sat for an hour in front of his typewriter, thinking. Drifting. He was rich and anonymous in a foreign city. He was playing thousands of roles. One day he was a poet, the next a dwarf carrying a poisoned stilletto, the next a ball of fire rolling through the main square of a working town, the next a suicide and on Friday he was a woman. With this thought he stayed. Was it hard to be a woman? He liked them better than men.

Kira came in with a dish of fried onions and a letter to her mother. She wanted him to add a few lines to her letter. He looked at the fried onions as in a mirror and, at length, he said:

–I want to be a woman.

–I don't think Mother would care much if you wrote that.

–But I do. Men are brutal, greedy, killers, and they make me sick. Take my own father. Much as I love him, all I really remember of him is his machine gun and his car.

–That's his cock. Why don't you just write: "The weather is fine. Kisses."

–I want to be a woman, he repeated stubbornly.

–Nothing easier, You made yourself into Andrei Codrescu . . . Why don't you make yourself into Maria . . . ?

–Maria Parfenie.

–Perfect. Maria Parfenie.

He was a beautiful woman in a splendid and free country. (She had to be beautiful!) Paris, Rome, London, New York, elegance, decadence, difference! Ideal photographs of places out of reach! Paradise regluttonized! What was he doing in this drab, military country where young men turned old before they had a chance to look? Where everything was enveloped in a brutal sense of self-importance and suspicion?

He began writing poems by Maria Parfenie. Every time he wrote *she* instead of *he*, he felt a deep physical thrill. Naturally, there was a woman in him. This woman could do a lot of things he wasn't allowed to do. She could, for instance, say: "I am crossing my legs and dreaming of China," something that wouldn't have occurred to his normal male self. Perversely and happily, Kira encouraged him. Physically, he saw this person as a combination of Kira and Alexandra. He filled two notebooks with marvelously inspired lines which he didn't even dare transcribe for fear that the collected emotion would kill him. When finally, he had Alexandra type the things up, she had a wild reaction.

–I don't write anything, she said, but this stuff makes me want to get up and dance.

So the three of them went dancing. And all the magazines published Maria Parfenie's poems and everyone wanted to know who she was. And he urged everyone, without telling them who Maria was, to change their identities, their sexes and their opinions. Become people in your imagination, he said when he got drunk, be like the Gypsies, tear up your identity cards! He got drunk often and he said many things. To top it all off, he realized that Maria Parfenie's force was purely feminine so he further separated her from the brutality of the kingdom of fathers and made her into a lesbian. And when this happened all the magazines stopped publishing her.

–I'm afraid, said Kira, that something is going to happen!

They were sitting by the window of their room watching the town light up for the evening. He felt chilly. He too had some premonitions. Between them was an empty bottle of cheap wine. Alexandra was asleep on the bed.

Kira had a cousin. His name was Eric and the reason he had never figured in their lives before was because he wasn't an intellectual. Or a bum. Or a poet. He was a muscle-boy who lay, most of the time, in his one room gym glistening with oil, covered by weights. His father was an embassy attaché who smuggled muscle magazines for him from the West. That was not all he smuggled. He also brought back records and tapes of the far-out new music from England and America, the Beatles and the Rolling Stones, and, seeing how Rumania was still in the fifties somewhere sobbing over the Loneliness of the Long Distance Runner, this new stuff was definitely incredible. He liked to rock back and forth, watching Kira and Alexandra dance. The wild rhythms took hold of him. Eric, who pretended to speak English, occasionally translated the songs and through it all, hedonistic energy poured into the room. Sometimes, Andrei would arrive from the Library where he had been reading an ancient mournful saga or a death liturgy and the music would penetrate the ancient texts he had just held and fill him with an energy so pure he felt the light exploding. He suspected now that somewhere out there, in the West, young people were exploring their bodies with all their

121

nerves. Eric's father, whom they met during one of his short return trips, unwillingly provided more fuel to the fire. He described the "horrors" of longhairs roaming the streets with guitars, hitchhiking, destroying their minds with drugs . . . Well, here was, Andrei thought, a sudden *mass* of poets . . . He'd always taken Rimbaud at his word about "the derangement of all the senses." What could be more marvelous than destroying one's mind? That mind which constantly adjusted and accommodated one to the zillion betrayals of society? To have a mind, so pure that only what mattered to the *body* would be experienced . . . He saw the giant figures of Meister Eckhart, Saint Theresa and Rimbaud rising from a musical marsh holding a giant sign: FUCK THE BOURGEOISIE! PROLETARIAN AND OTHERWISE!

Kira and Alexandra danced with each other. Eric moaned under the weights. Codrescu reflected. Maria Parfenie wrote poems and signed them with a heart. Yours truly. Andrei was so taken with the idea of drugs (he didn't know, at the time, that Rumanian peasants in Dobrogea had been smoking hashish for thousands of years) that he pretended to be stoned as he walked the streets or when he lay down. He shut his eyes, pummeled his temples with his fists, saw stars, his brain reeled, he felt weightless. Yes, he was as stoned as he would ever get. And he was happy. And he would get a headache and weight would return to the world. At the end of that summer, suddenly, the pain became intense and the world became heavier.

18

The Armed Forces, of which Alexandra had warned him a while back, caught up with him. He had always had an instinctive horror of uniformed people the way others have a horror of cats or insects. It wasn't something that he could control. It swept over him. Overtly, the reason had to do with the fact that he felt useless in the presence of a uniform. He had no place in the world of the uniform because, obviously, only other uniforms did. But there was also a visceral fear, gripping his throat. Perhaps this is why he hated Stoica. Stoica had submitted to the same mentality. The whole country, in fact, was ruled along the lines of army discipline. Everything had a strict place. He had no intention whatsoever of joining the army.

He looked at the green envelope some more and went out to find Kira. She was at Eric's. The ambassador was also there. He had just returned from Italy with a fresh load of records. Although he was itching to get Kira away, he stayed through a whole talk by His Excellency who, knotting his ferocious eyebrows, poured forth economic arguments mostly concerning the availability in Rumania of such things as Turringer salami, oranges, pâté de foie gras, etc., none of which were ever available. It was his ambition to make oranges a year-round thing in Rumania instead of the Christmas flash they were.

At length they said their goodbyes and he told Kira about the army when they got outside. She was stunned.
   –What are you going to do?
   –I don't know.

He did. Sort of. He wanted the two of them to leave the country, yet the practical difficulties seemed insurmountable. Exit visas were just not granted. There was one way, of course. If he applied for an emigration visa to Israel he could leave but they would certainly not allow Kira to come. Even so, he was only half-Jewish, the first time in his life when the "other" half counted for something . . . so he may not be able to leave at all.

Early next morning, they caught the express for Sibiu, leaving no address behind. As soon as they arrived in town, they went to see his mother, who was about to marry an X-ray technician. Mother was distressed. She wanted to go with him if he decided to leave. He reassured her. If worse came to worse and he *had* to leave, he would find some way to return soon.

He went to see Secretary Rana. Why Rana? He didn't know.
    Rana had aged. They talked about a thousand things. He could see that the local Secretary still had a soft spot for him ever since his "collar adventure." Rana knew everything about his expulsion and his subsequent adventures. He didn't know about the army. Feeling suicidal, he confessed his desire to leave the country. Rana was shocked.
    –What are you telling me this for?
    –Because I really don't know who else I should tell it to . . . and because . . . I don't really know who else could help me.
    –Help you?! You are absolutely out of your mind. . . .
    The Secretary's outburst frightened him.
    –Well, I am crazy, remember. . . .

But, instinctively, he had been right to see Rana. After long speeches, the Secretary promised that if he applied for an exit visa, he would see to it that the decision wouldn't be made at the lower levels. Andrei didn't know what he meant. He was struck by lightning next day when he found out that Rana, in his mania for extra positions had, not so long ago, named himself "security head of the militia's passport division," another extra salary.

124

Kira was crying. What could he do? They walked the melancholy streets, the air of which he knew so well. He knew, as did Kira, that she could not come with him. She was his wife, but the cruelty of the emigration policy was well known to both of them, and he could not afford to stay and fight it.

—Go, said Kira.

At the Militia Station, he filled in endless forms. So did Kira.

—What are you going to do?

—I'll fly back, she said. Wait. What else?

Her face took on the diamond shape he knew so well. For a moment they were both suspended there, in the town of his childhood with the great Teutsch Cathedral in the background. The impression stayed in the air and joined the other shadows. If you go there and wait, before sunset, you can still see it. They had come to a crossroad. The attractive future he had dreamed up, all the travel, poetry and adventure, paled. Kira, my sweet Kira, I don't want to leave. He looked around him for a sign. None came. What would his father have done in his place? He could not remember his father. He had made up so many fathers that now, when he needed real advice, no image came forth. The leather jacket fell off the shoulders of the picture in his head and the gun in the man's hand turned into a dry twig. It was a hot, somnolent afternoon. Kira leaned against him. There was nothing to say. Like the two brothers who came to a crossroad in the fairy tale, he wanted to ask her to plant a knife in the ground. He would do likewise and, years later, if they chanced upon the spot, they could see what had become of them. If the knives were rusted, their love had gone and one of them was dead.

A visa, even an emigration one, is not easily granted, and, in the feverish weeks that followed, he almost abandoned, many times, the idea of leaving . . . He almost went back to Bucharest, but he was wise not to. They were looking for him there.

He spent most of his time walking through the old haunts, marveling at the strength of his medieval town . . . he saw how Sibiu

125

had not exactly helped the Communists with his education . . . it was architecturally directed against the idea of heaven on earth . . . it was rotten baroque and ironic medieval . . . The Bruckenthal Museum, where he had spent days skipping school, had lost none of the magic it had given him. Old man Goldmutter, covered with gold as in Grandmother's pictures, stood at the entrance of it laughing, although his head was eternally split open with the iron ax. The windows, slanted like eyes, looked ironically on the world. If and when I return, he thought, I will be welcome here. Sibiu, like his childhood, was a permanent place because here he did not need to be a grown man. Here he could always dream.

The fateful day came. He was notified of approval. He flew back to Bucharest for the final papers.

He was processed in a long room with a long line of sad-looking people who were leaving everything to defy the absurdity of their lives and to see what was over the rainbow. At the Ministry of Internal Affairs, later, they made him sign a paper which said, in melodramatic and unnecessary language, that he was leaving forever and renouncing his Rumanian citizenship, and had no claim to anything or anyone he left behind.

It did not take him long to get ready. He didn't take books or poems (published or otherwise), only a few photographs and his clothes. Goodbye, lover, friend, wife! He was on his own.

Itt, Eric, Alexandra and Kira came to the airport. It was an awkward departure.

The small Al Italia jet crossed the border. In five minutes, he was in another world.

126

A LETTER

19

Italy has the magic of making potential things become manifest, my beloved Kira, and it is to you that this country is dedicated (in my head, anyway), because Italy is the story of your recession from wife to myth; the story of your reality becoming infused with the light of the Mediterranean until all that was left was an image, a primal image which I carry everywhere.

The light, to begin with, peels off one's concerns with the ease of a razor shaving a head. When you begin surrendering to this light, your essential qualities become manifest. Now bathe yourself in this light and imagine a race of ten-foot people hovering in the sky so that no matter where you stand in Naples, there is an enormous woman eating chocolate over your head, a car engine about to roll into the sky, lovers embracing in the air (which is warm and scintillating and languorous) and a variety of sentences in Italian ordering you to buy things and be happy. Advertisements are, naturally, the mark of the West and, when I look back at the drab and bare walls of our country, I have a hard time believing that I have lived so many years without color. These things are meant to, of course, make you spend your money (I have none but more about this later!) but, whatever their intentions, it is their color that predominates.

The Hotel di Napoli where we "refugees" are being housed is a rickety old thing near the waterfront. The Jewish Emigration Services which managed this housing for us would like to ship us to Israel immediately, a concern which, noble as it may be, doesn't sit with me because I plan to spend the rest of my days lying in the sun watching the ships, the street vendors (every conceivable trinket is for sale), the exuberant natives, the outdoor cafes, the blaring jukeboxes, but mostly the light. The light here is the key to the Renaissance, to everything.

Two weeks have passed. Yesterday they had an Israeli spy in the hotel who told everybody how marvelous life was in Israel and how everyone should go there. This is how things stand: Italy will not have us for more than six months (not Italy; the Italian Government) so everyone who does not want to go to Israel is now making a mad round to all the embassies that will have anything to do with us: Canada, USA, Australia, New Zealand, etc. I went to the Prefettura and asked to stay in Italy. They told me this wasn't possible unless I went to the university and that costs a great deal of money. I only have what the Jewish Services give me for pocket money which is enough for a biweekly trolley ride. They also pay for the hotel and two meals.

I was walking all over Naples thinking of various wild schemes to get rich fast, trying to learn from all the street operators who always seem to have something to sell. I'm picking up a fair amount of Italian, so yesterday I had my first real conversation with an Italian braggadocio who told me he makes five thousand lira a day smuggling cigarettes from the port into the city and then selling them on the streets. Mostly American cigarettes which are terribly expensive in the stores because of heavy duty. So, this morning, I wrapped myself in my long black windbreaker and went into the port to stroll around. A big ship full of American tourists had just come in. I followed my braggadocio friend at work and, imitating everything he did, I walked up to Americans, put on a smile and said: Cigarettes? Cigarettes? I collected about twenty-five assorted Marlboro, Kent and Winston cigarettes and then, trembling, I walked nonchalantly past the gate. I thought I was safe when I heard a port policeman behind me. "Aspetta!" he said, which means "Wait!" I didn't, obviously, wait. I broke into a run. I must have run for three kilometers before I stopped. And then came the selling part. I walked about fifteen times past a cafe before I dared go in.

130

Finally, I walked up to some seated people and said: "Cigarette Americano?" "Beat it," they said in English. They were Americans. I almost didn't go back to work. Well, it is now nine o'clock in the evening and I'm back. I sold six cigarettes: two Marlboros, three Kents and one Winston. I made exactly fifty lira which buys one cup of Espresso. I am through with this business. I have to think of something else.

Yes, I'm in Rome. I did get your last letter (the one in which you said: "My sweet fool, what are you doing selling cigarettes when you could be here leading the masses?") unless there was another letter . . . I must tell you how I got here. I met a Belgian dancer, Marcel, in a cafe. We talked about poetry and then I did some impromptu translations into French from this growing pile of poems about you. He loved them and said he would like to translate them into Italian. He was going to Rome to join up with the rest of his troupe (they are mimes doing a piece based on an Artaud poem) and offered to take me along and pay my way. Naturally, I went and here I am in this amazing city, sharing a room with Marcel in Piazza Vittorio Emanuele. Since we arrived two days ago, I've done nothing but walk all over Rome in a state of excitement which, combined with my love for you, conspires to make me completely insane.

Marcel, who is a mystic and a scholar also, has been showing me what he calls "secret Rome" . . . he is a student of alchemy and has figured out that many cathedrals and places here were built by alchemists at various times who meant to communicate great secrets through the layouts of their buildings.

I am writing a long poem called "From the River Aurelia" (your secret name) in which the women of the world finally leave all the men and build a civilization for themselves under the earth. In this underground paradise, there is harmony, a sense of lovely purpose, and artistic tempers flare and resolve themselves in music, while outside, on the earth's surface, the men, left to their own devices, make war on each other as blood and brutality reign. The men make themselves women out of salt and, with the help of these,

131

procreate. A new generation of half-flesh, half-salt children appears. War is their only reality. Woman is a dim memory. I don't know what I'm trying to do besides, obviously, idealize the natural superiority of the feminine principles out of which art and poetry are made, and, personally, I am suffering as if all women have disappeared from the earth . . . and they have. The poem goes on to describe the "singer" or the poet as a betrayer of man's sun culture who lives underground with the women who do not trust him because he is a man. I have, around me, Rome to support all my misery; Rome, the eternal city, where the sharpness of that conflict between man-the-destroyer and woman-the-creator has been refined, throughout the ages, and stares from every stone as a great mystery. The ideal androgyne, the solution of personality, was well known to these Romans. I saw a tombstone in Ischia which said: HERE LIES BURIED AUGUSTUS, FATHER, PRIEST AND HERMAPHRODITE.

In the very center of Rome (which is the center of the world) is the Forum, and in the center of the Forum there is a small shrine called UMBILICUS MUNDI, the navel of the world; a place which, by its position, links heaven, earth, and hell, and inside of which, if you sit there, a great energy, a wind of particles, charges you with power. Marcel pointed this spot out to me and it has become my favorite place. I sit inside for hours, healing my soul with these profound vibrations and dreaming of impossible places where all is peace, but mostly of you because you are the places where all is peace.

There are no ruins in Rome. Everything is exactly calculated to teach a mystery. Domus Aureus, the catacombs, the churches built on older churches, all these things are photographs of my soul.

I had a vision, last night (a dream?) in which you and Alexandra and I were sitting in a perfectly white room. A man came and showed us two pictures. One was a portrait of the Party Secretary. Over his face there were some Jewish letters. The other was a picture of a beautiful youth (of indeterminate sex). "You have to

132

tack one of these up," he said. Alexandra said: "Let's put up that young boy." You said: "Let's put them both up, just in case." I woke, feeling sad.

Apropos of what you said about our letters being opened and read . . . we have nothing to hide. This is something that was never clear to me in Rumania. I never knew why I had to stand up and say things. It wasn't, certainly, out of a great sense of justice. It was because there is nothing to hide.

Forgive me, love, for being such a lousy correspondent. A lot has happened.

Soon after my last letter, I was sitting on the Spanish Steps, in the sun, trying to avoid thinking about the end of the month when my visa expires. I noticed a small dark man walking back and forth.
    —Do you know Russian? he asked me.
    —Yes, I said, I am Rumanian.
    —Rumanian? My dear friend, he said in Rumanian, I think this is marvelous. My name is Willy. I am a Gypsy.

Willy had just received a long letter in Russian from one of his millions of relatives and needed someone to translate it. Willy does, in fact, speak thirteen languages, including Sanskrit and Arabic, but Russian just isn't one of them. He is the Bulibasha of a large tribe camped on the outskirts of Rome. Willy himself lives in the very posh center of Rome with his wife, who speaks only Romany, and their nine children. He makes a living, it seems, out of selling fake Persian carpets to gullible Italian housewives. He tells them that these are his last carpets and he must sacrifice them in order to return to Persia where his mother is dying. The Gypsies mass-produce these carpets. I don't think Willy needs to sell car- pets because he is very rich but he is an active Gypsy and he would feel strange without an "occupation" . . . Anyway, we went to a cafe and there I translated his letter for him, and then I told him about all my bureaucratic hassles. Willy laughed.
    —Five times, he said, spreading his fingers, I was thrown out of

133

Italy . . . three times I was thrown out of the U.S. . . . I can never go back to France . . . In Germany I can be arrested if I show up on the street. . . .

—What are papers? he continued philosophically. What is a name? I had fifteen or twenty names in five years . . . and see, I'm still the same person . . . I am a number . . . You want a passport? No problem. . . .

Willy held forth like this until it was time for dinner. We went to Il Rex Degli Amigi, a place that I'd seen but could never afford, and lingered over a gigantic meal for four hours.

What happened then creates a certain problem. I'm writing everything, love, because I have nothing to hide. I hope this won't offend you. It's so hard knowing exactly who we are and to what degree we depend on each other's lies. But I have decided to go on and here it is. . . .

We had finished our meal and, as we were about to leave, two beautiful black women sitting at the table on our left motioned Willy to come over. He did that . . . For a few moments, I was left alone, feeling marvelous . . . there was another half-bottle of wine. . . .

—Listen, said Willy when he came back, those girls invite us to their house for a little party. . . .

I haven't been doing too well in this department so I accepted gladly. The two girls exuded class. They were both as black as night and dressed as elegantly as I've ever seen anyone dressed. The older girl whose name was Maria drove a beautiful white Mercedes. We sat in the back as Willy, who is incapable of shutting up, explained in six languages at once that the world is a beautiful explosion of love, ideas, experience, etc., and only a fool would worry about papers and money. The other girl, Grazzia, looked at him with an amused smile. Maria reached into the glove compartment and pulled out a gold cigarette case. She opened it and pulled out a thin cigarette.

—Beautiful, Willy said, in English.

134

She lit the thing which smelled strange, inhaled deeply and passed it to Grazzia who did the same and gave it to Willy who also inhaled in a highly exaggerated manner and then handed it to me. I twisted it between my fingers, not knowing exactly what to do.

    –Smoke, said Willy, it's marijuana, Mary Jane, grass, weed, kif, bhang, cannabis. . . .

So that was it. Finally. I had, several times, approached the wild looking Dutch hippies on the Spanish Steps with the intention of asking for drugs but I never got up enough nerve to do it. I put the thin cigarette between my lips, sucked as hard as I could, and choked. Everybody laughed.

    –He's from behind the Iron Curtain, Willy said. They don't let him smoke there.

    –Love, said Maria, love behind the Iron Curtain.

I smoked as much of the thing as I could. I didn't feel any different but, for some reason, I couldn't take my eyes off a large sparkling sapphire on Grazzia's finger. The stone set off the most spectacular beams of light. Willy laughed. I laughed too. I felt light and happy and, I noticed, my laughter was of a quality unknown to me. They were all laughing. I was noticing the points where my laughter intersected with theirs to make a sort of big, happy splash like someone diving into water. And then, abruptly, I was terrified when I saw a giant globe of light go through the windshield. "No, no," I said. They all laughed hysterically. It was a street light. Everything bounced, floated and danced as I kept raising my index finger to my eye and saying, "One finger! One finger!" over and over again.

Not long after, we were inside a large apartment with glass chandeliers floating from the ceiling, pillows on the floor, carved ivory masks, and African sculpture. A long time must have gone by, a time during which I had been absorbed by a feathered figure exuding, simultaneously, a great amused wisdom, terrific cruelty and an unbearable sensuality.

    –That's Kakunga from the Congo, said Maria. He likes to watch people fuck.

135

In the middle of the floor sat a big water pipe with mouthpieces hanging from it. Grazzia put hashish in the bowl and we each took one of those in our mouths and smoked.

—Hashish, Willy's voice came from somewhere, is why Gypsies are so smart . . . they never settle for anything. . . .

Maria had changed, somehow, into a transparent silk sarong and Grazzia took off all her clothes, crossing her legs and staring straight into my eyes. I don't know when and how we started to move but I remember this tableau:

My body, perfectly white, lies still on its back as four black hands are undulating on it in a complex rhythm. We formed, at this point, an organic piano. After this still, things acquired great speed and the imminent orgasm which had set off small explosions in my body, came. It was a tremendous tearing apart of the universe. I came for what seemed like twenty years.

And thus it came to pass that, for three weeks I did not (could not, was not allowed to) leave this house and I was a white harem slave of two black sultanas. Not only did Maria not allow me to leave the house, but when I told her I was going to, she took away my watch and hid it. A variety of people went in and out of the house during the days of my "confinement." There was Claude, a seventeen-year-old French boy, pretty as a girl, who had never before made love to a woman and who, finally, fell so madly in love with Grazzia that he had to be gotten rid of by buying him a car . . . (Maria thought nothing of the expense.) Roy, the black American jazz musician, brought with him a number of jazz records and a whole range of sexual techniques which he demonstrated to (and with) everyone during his two-day sojourn. One of his specialities was called buzzing and it was a way of vibrating a clitoris (or a penis) in the manner of playing a trumpet. Claire, the Italian girl who was a shoe saleslady on Via Venetto, could make two men and two women come simultaneously through a variety of perfectly timed tongue, hand, and fuck movements. I received a thorough education here.

136

I was, frankly, fantastically tired after three weeks, and I planned to escape, watch or no watch. But this wasn't necessary because Maria announced one evening: "It was pleasant knowing you all but now we have to say goodbye because our husband returns from Somalia tomorrow morning. . . ."

The ambassador did, apparently, return, because yesterday Willy and I tried to pay a visit, and were met at the door by an Italian maid who said: "Madame ambassador is not receiving anybody."

As a parting present, Maria gave me a little white pill which, she said, I should take when I wanted to write my greatest poem.

When I got back here, Marcel was worried. He almost didn't believe my story of drugs and abduction. And then he handed me all these letters from you, my dear Kira.

I've just written all this, as honestly as I could, and I don't know if I should send you the letter. I feel guilty. Not about what I did (which means perhaps that I have no inborn moral sense) but about the great contrast between our lives at this point. I know that all my affairs, at this point, must seem strangely frivolous to you. You are, no doubt, studying hard for the trigonometry and calculus exams, thinking of me, seeing the same old creepy faces and the banners full of slogans and the boring newspapers. I'm a horrible brute.

Two days have gone by, Kira, . . . I love you.

My visa has expired. Willy said it was a simple matter.
  —Where do you want to be from? he asked.
  —From Persia, I said.

I didn't leave the house all day yesterday for fear that the carabinieri might stop me and ask for papers. My hair has grown very long (I haven't cut it since leaving Bucharest) and there is a campaign against cappelloni (longhairs) in Rome. Marcel, who is also a yogi,

showed me some basic postures and taught me things about chak-
ras and the kundalini. He will soon leave for India to study with
a Tibetan master. The day passed quickly and two hours ago Willy
came with my new Persian passport. It is a phenomenal thing.
Between these thick covers, printed with letters I don't understand,
is my freedom from bureaucracies. I can go anywhere except, of
course, to Persia. When I asked Willy about the price, he merely
waved his hand in the air and said it was a gift from one wanderer
to another. The photograph on the document is, by the way, my
Lyceum graduation picture. I had no other.

Sweet Kira, I hope the postmark doesn't shock you. I am in Paris,
yes, in fabulous Paris. I should, I guess, start this chronologically
although I'm not sure if there really is a chronology.

After Willy brought me my new passport, we celebrated with wine
for a short time and then I went out by myself, feeling my brand
new identity solidly stuck on the inside of my shirt. I felt so brash,
in fact, I wished that a policeman would stop me so I could pull
out the document and present myself in this new form, a form
without history. Looks like I am doomed to forever changing iden-
tities. Instead, I took the little white pill that Maria gave me and
sat down on the edge of the Fontana Trevi.

Something was happening to me. The afternoon sun fell on my
hand turning it to gold. It didn't look like gold. It was gold. Of
course, I thought, I am made out of gold. I looked at my other
hand. It too had turned to gold. I unbuttoned my shirt and stared
down at my puny chest from which those three hairs were still
undecided whether to fall off or not. My chest was a solid sheet
of gold. I knocked on it with both fists and in that muffled thud
I heard all kinds of voices, whispers really, coming from very far,
from my blood, saying: GOLD! EVERYTHING IS GOLD!
YOUR BLOOD IS MADE OUT OF GOLD! For a moment I
thought that I had been attacked, from the inside, as it were, by
old man Goldmutter who was sending an advance load of gold
before introducing me to my fate . . . but I dismissed the thought

when I looked at the water of Fontana Trevi leaping and exploding fancifully in zillions of particles of gold which floated in the air and touched the tourists who walked about, uncomprehending, not seeing the miracle. Fools! they jangled their stupid cameras and talked loudly without noticing for a second that their bodies were made out of shimmering gold. I looked around, love, and everything in the world, the stones, the church, the old lady leaning out the window, the street signs, the angry man who walked cursing around his stalled car, everything, everything, was made of this same stuff I was . . . living, playful, marvelous myriads of interlocking gold cells dancing . . . The bells of the Santa Maria Maggiore tolling the hour, the honking of car horns, the voices, everything I heard, became material, composed of this stuff . . . of course . . . It was all so obvious. I saw you, Kira, and all our friends and all my past which, somehow, wasn't a "past" at all, and I looked at the Communist Party and at the trees and they too and you with them lived and breathed in the same substance . . . made from this same substance, this essence of . . . light . . . of course, the world was made out of light . . . the universe was made out of light . . . I grabbed my hair and pulled it with the joy of this discovery . . . the pain too was gold . . . I wanted to shout, to tell everyone immediately about it . . . How could they not know . . . It is so obvious . . . SO OBVIOUS!! SO FUCKING OBVIOUS! This is what Maria had meant by my "greatest poem" . . . it was . . . And it was not only my greatest poem but everyone else's greatest poem . . . everyone and everything participated, joined irreversibly in this poem . . . the whole universe was this poem and how could anyone fail to SEE? It was funny . . . it was hysterically funny . . . I laughed loudly, in waves, in ripples, in dots, in stripes, watching my laughter dissolve in light . . . how stupid . . . What was everyone so worried about? What was everyone's problem? Blindness . . . Blindness . . . There was no death . . . the whole amazing universe was vibrating, alive. . . .

I left Fontana Trevi, jumping, dancing with delight. I had never felt this kind of joy. I LOVE EVERYONE ALIVE! . . . There is nothing bad . . . evil does not exist.

I found myself, hours later, sitting on the steps of Santa Maria Maggiore, weeping for joy, eating a big fat red juicy apple . . . How did this apple get to me? How did this incredible, powerful, happy apple come to me? Thank you, apple, I kept saying as I bit huge chunks out of it, thank you, apple, for letting me eat you, thank you tree for making this apple, thank you Eve for eating this apple . . . thank you Eve for fucking Adam in his gold blindness . . . thank you, thank you . . . I ate the whole apple, the little spine included, and I became an apple myself. Eat me, I said to the sad looking people going in for confession, eat me, I am a big, fat, juicy apple . . . I saw that all that was in my "past" was with me at all times and the "future" was too and you, Kira, were me . . . I was free, FREE!!

I got back to Marcel's somehow and I spent what remained of the night kissing and embracing my friend who, not knowing what was happening, but suspecting a deep religious revelation, held me tightly and listened.

Next day I felt weary yet fresh. I felt as if all fear had been torn from me. I packed my bag the same day and said my goodbyes. A bus took me to Autostrada del Sole *(Highway of the Sun!) and I stuck my thumb out, feeling no identity, no roots, no regrets . . . I had been washed clean. I didn't care where I was going.*

I won't tell you all the details of this hitchhiking trip because there are too many. In my newly found state I was paying attention to everything. I felt aware of millions and millions of things. The universe, I realized, is a novel written from the point of view of every single thing in it. It was enough to drive one crazy. I arrived in Paris three or four days later. On the road, somewhere, I hooked up with an American girl, Amina, who had a bag full of poetry books and no money. I had none either and our day of absolute misery came in a little town in Tuscany. We had to get food. I went to the Communist newspaper in town and I said: "I am from Rumania. I would like to write an article about how wonderful life is over there." They threw me out. Next, I went to the Fascist newspaper (they have one of each) and I said: "I am a refugee from

Rumania. I would like to write an article about Communist horrors." They didn't want it either but the editor was understanding. He gave us 5,000 lira. We ate and then got a ride out of there, in the rain, in a hearse, sitting in the back with the bouncing coffin. Next, a truck full of clams took us to France.

Anyway, we are in Paris. Paris is everything I thought Paris would be. You know the common saying about absent-mindedness in our country: "He's in Paris!" Well, it couldn't have been said any better. Going into rapture over it, this little Rumanian, plus Amina, circled every cafe on the left bank, reciting every French poem in his head but mostly: "Il pleut sur les toits/comme il pleut dans mon coeur," although it was a perfectly sunny day and everyone had an ice cream cone in his/her hand. I immediately thought of calling on all our famous compatriots in Paris but I had neither the credentials nor the appearance necessary. My pants were torn in six places, my shirt was almost nonexistent, and Amina looked like a child-whore in Les Miserables. *We had a cup of coffee in* Les Deux Magots. *This was the last of our collective money but Amina expected her folks in New York to appear at any moment in the form of a check at the American Express office.*

This check did, indeed materialize, but only two days later, two days which we spent sleeping on a table at the Zero cafe, a place owned by the mother of one of Amina's friends. But I was happy sleeping on the table. I looked at the Italian poems I had written, now that I had gained a certain distance from Italy, and saw that Italian was definitely not my language. It is a beautiful language to talk in and a miserable language to write in. An unnerving sing-song penetrates its syllables, a terribly romantic, sentimental softness which is lovely in songs and unbearable in poems. Ungaretti, the one poet to take Italian by its poetic horns, wrote poems so short they can't sing. I burned the entire pile. I looked also at the few French poems I had written. These were, in many ways, worse. This language is like a piece of French pastry, full of stratified stylistic clichés. These are not obvious linguistic clichés, they are civilized traps into which one falls unwittingly. To break through the French language and come up fresh is an effort either

141

for a madman or for a supreme academic. Artaud and Queneau.
I really admire Cioran for writing such an elegant French, for being
such a combination of the two. But it isn't for me. So I burned this
pile too, leaving only what I already sent you, the long "River
Aurelia."

Well, Amina's check came and the following days were orgiastic.
   God! Going through restaurants and having things like Chinese
Duck on Snow, which is duck spread apart on dayglo Chinese
snow, and snails, which are these small animals boiled in garlic
that explode when you close your mouth, and carved brains of lamb
which come in the shape of Venetian gargoyles, and, finally, fish
eyes and goat balls fried in olive oil and soaked in Portuguese wine.
To which we added our own menus, things like hearts of lamb, dog,
chicken, rats and rabbits served on round antique mirrors; fish-and-
chips wrapped in Xerox copies of menus from Town & Country;
salads seasoned with the sperm which Amina managed to milk out
of me right before dinner; black bread spread thick with caviar with
an oyster staring from the middle of it like a carnivorous vagina;
all red meals which went from borscht to pomegranates; whole
lambs stuffed with whole chickens, and so on, ad nauseum, at the
end of which Amina went back to hamburgers and swore never to
stray again. All this from ONE check? you may ask. That ONE
check was for 3,000 dollars, and That's A Fact.

You must see this orgy, Kira, on the background of all the great
paintings I looked at during those two weeks. The Louvre, which
is like a polished magic mirror out of which every fantasy appears
with the help of an extra sense of direction, even has a marvelous
portrait of you by Ingres. I looked at it until I was thrown out of
the museum. I don't know what is happening to me; I don't know
where I am pushed and why and it does not, basically, matter. But
seeing you made me feel sad again. What is this violence inside
that makes us love?

To get on with the story, my birthday came (as it does) and Amina
threw a little party. She was, at this time, falling in love with a
permanently stoned blonde who flipped his long hair from the right

142

to the left every three seconds. It's amazing, dear Kira, how easily promiscuous Amina is. I am told that all American girls are. This is interesting, if true, because I think monogamy is ridiculous. But, of course, Amina is rich and, due to this, she may behave differently from the rest of the mortals. There was a lot of grass at the party. Everyone was stoned. During the general confusion, someone spoke of recently having taken LSD. I told him about my experience in Rome. Yes, he said, that was pure Sandoz. Oh, love, do you know what this means? It means that my Universe of Gold is within everyone's reach. Amazing, indeed.

LSD.

Time came for the presents. There were a few curious things, a bunch of books and a plain envelope. I opened this first, suspecting that it contained hashish. But no. In this envelope was an airplane ticket with a fill-in-your-own-name blank at the top. It said PARIS-NEW YORK. One way. TWA. I was speechless with contradictory emotions. On one hand, I felt absolutely thrilled. On the other, I was shocked. Why would Amina spend so much money on me? I looked at her. She smiled mysteriously. I realized that, perhaps, she had not been wholly responsible for it. In my Universe of Gold, a giant dancing hand guides everything. And she had received the divine slap. And the blonde fellow was, of course, happy to see me go. . . .

Do I want to go to America? Should I go to America? From all I know about it, I could as well go to China. I don't know the language. I have heard nothing about the natives except that they smile dazzlingly and bang their Cadillacs into one another. American poetry is unknown to me. I have read all the novels. I've seen a lot of movies. And there is Vietnam. Every day, since I came West, I have heard about the massacres the Americans are daily committing in Vietnam. Do I really want to go there?

I do.

My sweet Kira . . . I think I've just taken another marriage vow. I have exactly fifteen dollars. I will write you from New York. Seems like I am always leaving. . . .

BOOK THREE

20

All kinds of people had gone, before him, to America for specific purposes. Tourists, as a rule, don't go to America. Businessmen do. Emigrants do. Poets don't. Poets leave America. So what kind of a perverse destiny pushed him there? he thought, as he listened to the three Yugoslavs behind him eating onions, wiping their mouths and saying every two seconds: "America! America!" (These Yugoslavs were on the wrong plane. They had missed their special charter flight and were going TWA instead.) Michaux had been to America. Cendrars starved in New York for awhile, just long enough to write his great "Easter in New York." On second thought, all kinds of poets had been to America. But they had all been victims of historical circumstances. He was the first, as far as he knew, to go to America because his girl friend wanted to get rid of him.

–Do you have anything to declare, Mr. (. . .)?

That's a good one. He went through a quick mental inventory of his personal belongings: two pairs of socks, two pairs of pants, a hat, a pair of blue gloves, a razor, the clothes on him. Were these things really his? They had all been given to him with the exception of the blue gloves which he had bought out of the money for an article on Rumanian poetry he had written for *Les Lettres Francaises*. No, they were not really his. On lease. His poems . . . a thick sheaf of poems . . . no, not really. Compliments of the Muse. His name? Well, this is, naturally, a good one. What is the name on that passport, anyway? A woman? No, he doesn't own a woman. It would be nice to have one, of course. A skinny

147

blonde woman. Then his body, his body must surely be his. He could leave it to medical research. Yes, his body is his. Although he isn't completely sure that this notion does not originate in the brain . . . yes, of course the brain thinks it owns the body . . . no, no, sir.

—Nothing to declare. I own nothing.

A clean slate.

So this was New York. Squares of sky sat between vertical slices of glass. Advertisements loomed enormous and burst forth with every kind of proposition imaginable: all was permitted, all was, in fact, necessary. The furiously rushing population caught him in swirls. He had grown short. The tall Americans, lunging headfirst into the subways, seemed filled with apocalyptic energy.

He had just spent seven of his fifteen dollars on a taxi which took him from Kennedy Airport to "Graynwich Village" (accent on "a"), as he pronounced the two out of the six English words he knew.

Of all varieties of cultural shock, the kind that hit him was the most pleasant. It synchronized, in a split second, his fantasies with the reality of the streets around him, as they looked that afternoon in Greenwich Village. Not all that hair (though, certainly, hair is an angelic musical instrument), not the beads around the necks, not the air of unmistakeable sensuality (though certainly yes), not the general abandoned weirdness of the population (yes yes), not the colored sign beaming messages translating, in short: EVERY-THING GOES! YOU ARE FREE!, not that, but *in* that: the promise of a brain transplant! He had no way of knowing that for every original, ten thousand copies lurked around; he couldn't know that America was an uninterrupted anthology of fads chasing each other faster and faster across shorter and shorter time spans. He thought that everyone on the street was a poet or an artist and that, somehow, here was the freedom to be anyone he wanted to be.

148

Dinner, in an Italian restaurant, took another four dollars out of his remaining eight.

Walk, walk, walk. Where did these people get their inexhaustible energy? From a sense of possibilities, no doubt. But then, how was it that for every human failure there was a neon sign? Lonely? There is a sign that said LONELY. Hungry? There is a sign that said HUNGRY. Did these signs make anyone less lonely or hungry? Instead of explaining or fulfilling needs, these signs seemed to be accusations of some sort: YOU ARE LONELY! YOU ARE HUNGRY! Then the idea struck him that a democracy is, essentially, an acknowledgment of the banality of collective needs. So far so good, he thought, but what do the poets have to say about it?

As he rested his weary body at a table in Le Figaro, corner of Bleeker and MacDougal, he closed his eyes and saw the big airport clock proclaiming, for the record, this message: March 13, 1966. This date circled in his head, filling him with vigor as the waitress brought him his third cup of espresso.

–March 13, 1966, he whispered.

–In America, dogs walk about with pretzels on their tails, said Grandmother from the dim past.

There were no poets in the cafe, only two Frenchmen at the next table. They were "emigrants." They were going to make a pile of money, they said, go back to France and open a pinball cafe. The Frenchmen had all kinds of ingenious ways to make money in the U.S. One of these was the Sperm Bank. One could, apparently, donate the milky stuff for a cool and quick fifty bucks. The Sperm Bank was somewhere on Columbus Avenue, the younger one said, adding that he would rather die than pass on his bad genes. He was an existentialist.

His four dollars, which had now become $2.75, did not get him a hotel room but that was no problem because the benches in Washington Square Park, though cold, were the right size. Dur-

149

ing the night, in connection with the Sperm Bank, he had several delicious dreams in which a miniskirted nurse took hold of his prick and, by means of an expert hand job, emptied him into a glass tube. The tube itself was a vast glass building with thousands of handsome people sitting at their desks with their mouths open.

In reality, the Sperm Bank was on the Avenue of the Americas, so he spent most of the following morning walking up to dignified businessmen and elegant ladies, and asking, "Where is the Sperm Bank, please?" There must have been many quick replies because he remembers a tangle of amused smiles, but finally, a Red Cross nurse directed him to the place.

The road was paved with temptations, the walls were covered with messages, the angry cars screamed, the buses smelled like perfume and shoes, and the people looked either insane or terrified. The fat male doctor (who spoke French) questioned him on the facts of his racial history. Unfortunately, he remembered his present identity. His "Arab Stock" did not make a great impression on the Doc.

    –Frankly, he said, we have very few requests for Persian stock. Occasionally, we get a request or two for Eastern European stock but it's a touch-and-go matter.

    "Touch-and-go," which Doc said in American, added themselves to his vocabulary which had already grown to the size of a small orange.

His sperm, which his ancestors had concocted to make themselves immortal, was not needed. He should have seen, in this, a clue to the fact that it is possible to be someone else up to a point.

He told the doctor his financial troubles. The $2.75 from last night had become, after a few more cups of coffee, exactly $1.36.

    –Take my advice, the man said, and go back to Persia . . . this place is horrid without money.

    Out of his own pocket, Doc removed five dollars, gave it to him, and then, closing the door said:

    –The bank might not use your sperm but I sure could.

150

With these words he fell on his knees and, without further ado, sunk his lips on the hero's cock and enriched his private bank with a beautiful amount of come. To leave no doubt that this was preferable, he added that the *official* method of extraction at the bank consisted in having a painful electrode shoved up the anus.

This is more than ambiguous, America, he thought to himself as two lines formed immediately in his head:

> Officially, stock worthless.
> Privately, worth five dollars.

There was only one kind of person who could explain to him the nature of America's welcome. A poet. He had to find a poet. He had, in his notebook, the address of the most American of all poets. He decided to call on him.

His first glimpse of the Lower East Side filled him with delight. The happy inhabitants cramming in and out of delis jammed with meats and cheeses, made him happy. The building he was looking for was a horrible, decaying structure, peeling slowly in the pale March sun. A large Puerto Rican family sat on the steps drinking beer.

–Does Allen Ginsberg live here? he asked.

–Never heard of him, they answered all at once, after some deliberation.

He walked into the dark hallway, barely lit by a cruddy lightbulb, and checked rows of mailboxes, many of which had been torn open with teenage screwdrivers. Sure enough, one of them said: Allen Ginsberg/Peter Orlovsky. Amazing! He had been sure that anybody as famous must be known by every child. He knocked on the door. After a long wait (during which he had decided to say, if asked, "A great Rumanian poet!"), the door opened. A fantastically skinny, ethereal being stood there, stark naked, water dripping from his ribs.

–Come in. I'm Peter Orlovsky, he said.

–Speak to me in the bathroom, said Peter. I've been spending all my time in the tub.

151

He sat on the edge of the bathtub as Peter resubmerged himself. They didn't talk because Peter said nothing, He wandered into the kitchen. Two people, who looked like even skinnier replicas of Peter, sat transfixed on chairs staring into the void. There was no answer to his "Hello." After a few minutes, however, they both turned around and fixed their collective gaze on the zipper of his parka. He felt uncomfortable but as time wore on, he relaxed. This is the house of a poet, he thought, and no matter what bizarre things go on, this is my only hope of finding out why America is the way it seems to be.

He was immensely relieved when Allen came home. He recognized him from photos but, even if he hadn't, the man's familiarity was electric. He was jovial, hospitable, and shook his hand as if he had expected him. He offered Andrei a glass of milk. The poet moved all over the room in a flurry of movement, pulling books out of shelves, showing him album covers, poems and newspaper articles, speaking fast (in French) about people and events which, up to this point, had been veiled in legend for him. He said Kerouac, Cassidy, San Francisco, Prague, Andrei Vosnesenski, pot and Umberto Saba in one sentence. He had a lovely voice. The two skinny men sat unmoved under the umbrella of Allen's words, never taking their eyes off his zipper. Two skinny girls came in, talked to each other, left.

They went out and had lunch in an ancient Jewish place on Avenue B. Ginsberg was well known here and the man behind the counter, who could have been his grandfather, addressed a rapid barrage of Yiddish at him. As soon as they were finished, the poet grabbed a bagful of rice pudding for Peter, paid, and walked out the door.

Back at the house, Allen gave Peter his pudding, and started to pack. He put a box of incense cones, a bundle of incense sticks, some finger cymbals, three books in a small packing case. Andrei watched in awe. People walked in and out of the house. Albert Fine came in and the talk turned to painting. Allen chanted in Sanskrit.

–See you kids, he said. I'm off to India.

152

Later, walking up the dark streets with Albert Fine, who had offered him a room for the night, he clutched tightly at the bundle of books Ginsberg had given him and tried to collect his thoughts. He couldn't. Instead of falling into place, America had pushed him out of his place. He felt dazed. Everything remained a mystery. He was beginning to lose his familiarity with himself.

21

Sometimes a man needs a heavenly protector. At other times he needs only his ego to legitimize his impulses. At other times, he is merely in need of money. He was in need of all three but money was the most urgent.

Signor Giuseppe Gherardi Verdi Manzzini of the Napoli Pizzeria on 53rd or 56th, frowned and said in Italian, in answer to Andrei's question in Sicilian:
    –Sure, we can use a dishwasher.
    –How much?
    –Well, let's see, mused Giuseppe . . . you can't speak English . . . you can't make pizza . . . 50¢ an hour.

That was fine. That is, everything was fine until monumental towers of dishes toppled his way . . . towers which his coworker, a giant Negro, danced out of the air by magical means and wiped clean in tenths of a second. The second day on the job, Signor Giuseppe suddenly appeared from the dining room where he doubled as a waiter and told him that the former delivery boy ("a goddamned spic") had just disappeared with the day's take and Codrescu had been elected to take his place. Relief! No more dishes!

His first delivery found him walking across 56th in a long, tomato-stained apron, carrying a hot square box (the circle in the square). The door he had knocked on opened after a while but only as far as an inside latch would allow. He tilted the pizza so it would fit and gave it to the man, peering through the crack. The door shut with a bang, then a hand reappeared and gave him some money. He counted it. There was not enough. He knocked again. The door recracked. "Not much?" he said. The man ran back and returned with a revolver which he stuck on the warm tip of his own nose.

–The pizza's all smashed up, bum, he said.

He ran downstairs. There is no way a pizza can be delivered horizontally through a crack in the door, Dear God!

When he returned, Il Padrone pointed with evil glee at a pile of pizzas and said,

–The girls want twenty pizzas.

It was the first time he had ever carried twenty steaming hot pizzas, each one its own volcano, and his steps were shaky. He arrived at the building bent in two and sweating. The door he was looking for opened and a completely naked woman stared at him. "Come, look at this, girls!" she shouted, and now twenty naked girls rushed toward him to see the sight. This was more than he could handle and, with a gesture replete with visions of his tomato-stained apron, he dropped the whole throbbing load of mushrooms, sausages, and anchovies at their feet. The boxes opened and the stuff exploded. A spastic cloud of laughter from the audience enveloped him all the way back after he had wiped the mess with his apron, which he had torn, furiously, from his waist.

–You're a good-for-nothing, said Signor Giuseppe, I will make a man out of you.

–I will kill somebody, he said in German. Instead, he wrote a poem.

America was both very dangerous and hysterically funny. How those two combined, and why, was something he had to look into next. He didn't have to wait long.

Signor Giuseppe made him, on the third day, into a Pizza Maker. This hallowed status was arrived at after the former Pizza Maker had vanished with the secret recipe.

–A goddamned wop, said Signor Giuseppe, who spared nobody. Making pizzas wasn't easy. One flips the rolled dough through the air until a perfect circle forms and then the thing is dropped abruptly on the table with a flick of the wrist. From the beginning, he could make nothing but square pizzas. He had made about twenty of these when Signor Giuseppe walked in and cut short his euphoria with the words: "YOU EAT THESE!" He also handed him five dollars in parting money, while Codrescu's eyes, smarting from pain, looked at him in an indescribable mixture of condolences and endless pity. "GO JOIN THEM!" he added, pointing to a throng of demonstrators blocking traffic on their way to the UN building.

He did. He joined them with his armload of square pizzas, grinding his teeth and saying "Fuck it" in many languages. His appearance was greeted with great joy by the demonstrators who were starving from shouting HEY, HEY, LBJ, HOW MANY KIDS DID YOU KILL TODAY? and soon, some two hundred people marched on eating a slice of pizza with Codrescu in front, waving his tomato-stained apron and reciting Rimbaud.

Leslie, who got no pizza, but was highly amused by his appearance, attached herself to him and, together, they experienced for the first time, the heart throb that goes with having a thousand cops thrust sticks in your face. Yes, he thought, this place is simultaneously funny and dangerous so the only recourse for a thoughtful person is to, likewise, become funny and dangerous. He was funny, all right, but he just wasn't dangerous.

Leslie lived in a crashpad on the Lower East Side, not far from Ginsberg's place, and they went there. On his way to her bed, he stepped on several cloudy bodies shimmering in candle light as Dylan rocked the place saying, "freedom's just another word for nothing left to lose."

Leslie had a brutal way of making love and, later, as he fell asleep, she read him her poetry from long sheets of colored paper. He didn't sleep long. The door blew off the hinges of the apartment

156

across the hall and what seemed like an army of police filled the building.

–They're coming here next, said Leslie, pulling her jeans on. Everyone was of the same opinion. They didn't bother to put out the candles. They filed out and walked, fast, to a car parked on the sidewalk.

–We leave New York until things cool off, said Leslie.

–OK, said Bob, who owned the car. There were nine of them in the Oldsmobile. It was warm. He fell asleep.

He woke in the dark. Leslie slipped him a tab of acid. He took it.

For a long time, they glided through upstate New York. Dark shapes floating out the window told him that spring was coming. It was a full moon, Bob Dylan was on the radio. And Bob Dylan, the second poet to talk to him, sang in Rumanian. It was a beautiful but sad song. It told him that he had been orphaned. That language is one's mother and when she is abandoned, she takes the soul with her. He must find another. Why have a mother? he asked and Bob Dylan said: "Because without her the pirates will destroy you." He knew five languages. Were they all his mother? Was he the child of a collective? Languages, like mothers, can get restricting. And you leave them looking for one that will accommodate your fantasies. Your self, as such, gets restricting, too. So you find another. Language and self are the carefully coded means of control whereby an alien thing controls the world. To what purpose? To deprive us of humanity. Why? "Because," Dylan said, "humanity is a natural resource which the aliens need to eat. They eat vibes." It was quite a song.

Then someone asked where we were going and, it turned out, they were going to Detroit. Hello, Celine. Detroit it was.

157

22

"I know what you need
Only
because you don't know what you want,"

said the jukebox in the Artist's Workshop in Detroit. Fantastically dressed characters floated in and out of the joint, waving multicolored rags at a girl with tatoos on her legs who did yoga on the sidewalk under the trembling of a saxaphone blown by a black man. Swarms of underage boys and girls, fresh out of the rich and bored suburbs of Detroit, reclined against surrealistic objects, passing joints and pointing in glee at acid-colored flies diving for their hair. John Sinclair, the queen bee, emerged occasionally from his upstairs apartment and bestowed blessings upon the crowd. He had just emerged from jail where he had been put for the generous crime of handing a joint to a cop. His locks had been shorn. That was the same cop, incidentally, who busted him twice before on the same charge and was as time rolled on, to bust him three more. It is better, of course, to hand five joints to the same cop.

Leslie looked around for a place to crash. She found Jimmy Black. Jimmy Black took them home where he lived with Mildred Muffin. Jimmy was gay and Mildred weighed 600 pounds, so they lived together chastely in a fairy tale full of psychedelic toys, kaleidoscopes, basic models of the universe in clay and papier mâché, bits of glass, mirrors, rolls of red, purple and black velvet and mannequins of all descriptions.

The acid he'd taken began to work, and he found himself in a long dark hallway at the end of which a strobe light could be seen spewing Jim Morrison's inspired words: "Father, I want to kill you! Mother I want to. . . . ! !" into the thick air. The hallway itself was really an amniotic passage through which he was propelled on his way to being born. He was crawling and things were going smoothly when a side door opened and a vast, dark Someone threw a glass of water in his face. Thank you, Father, he said, and plunged into the sea or lake which was in his way. He swam like this for hours and, finally, got to the light at the end of the tunnel just as Morrison said: "Break on through to the other side!" This, he had done. Father is dead, he decided, and Mother is a mystery. I am not looking for comfort any longer. I am looking for an explanation.

John Coltrane was on the turntable. The editor of the *Fifth Estate* (the underground newspaper) was telling John Sinclair about the antiwar demonstration scheduled for that afternoon. A hundred people were expected to demonstrate but the BREAK-THRUS (local Fascisti) planned to beat everybody up. Something had to be done. John was nonviolent.

–Give them acid, he said.

The editor was exasperated.

–They are coming down with rocks and clubs, John. . . .

–Sing OM, said John.

The editor left.

–Everybody is so busy in America, said Codrescu.

–Yeah.

Soon the room was filled with the MC5, the local rock'n roll band. They were having trouble booking a room because they were so loud. John made a telephone call. They could have the room. A skinny black man, who had just run a new "free poem" on the downstairs mimeograph, passed copies around. It was one of John's poems, called, typically: "Listening to John Coltrane." He read it. Didn't understand a word.

–This is a French poet, said John to the black man.

–Do you want to read with us at the concert? he said.

159

—I don't write English very well.
—Who cares? Read in French.

Detroit was not New York . . . Miles and miles of desolate and abandoned factories pierced the grey murky sleet . . . Teeming ghettos possessed by amazing energy . . . cars . . . cars . . . cars . . . Staring at the river of cars flowing under him, from the bridge over John Lodge Expressway, he realized the Law of Cars . . . the endless stream of machines rolling under him had a pattern . . . red cars always followed red cars . . . bursts of red cars appeared suddenly . . . yellow cars followed yellow cars . . . fleets of white cars sticking together like hives exploded horizontally past him . . . and so on . . . There certainly was a will behind these machines, a technological monster, licking its paws. . . .

He took buses. On the Dexter bus, he asked the driver:
—Can I buy the Dexter bus? (meaning, can I *ride* it).
The busdriver pushed him roughly down the stairs and said:
—Go buy the Livernois bus!

These buses took him everywhere. He got on them at random. One time, a bus took him into the deserted downtown area. It was evening. He walked into a greasy something called a Luncheonette. Two men with straw hats leaned on the jukebox . . . the light was dim and the dark waitress with huge breasts wiped aimlessly at a greasy counter with a yellow rag. . . .
—Cafe, he said.
—What?
—Cafe.
—What's he saying, Charles?
A groan came from under the counter.

He grabbed her hand (a most irrational gesture!) and pointed it to the coffee pot resting half full on the hot plate in front of her.
She shrieked.
—Charles! A sexual maniac grabbed me!!

160

This time, the groan increased and a shirtless black giant emerged from under the counter.

–WHAT DO YOU WANT? he said in a very big voice.

Exasperated, he pointed to the coffee pot and said, "CAFE!"

Then he pointed to the giant and said, "BLACK!" and then pointing to himself, he said "NO SPEAK ENGLISH!"

–He wants a cup of coffee, Rosalie, and don't be so damned rash.

He got his cup of coffee.

Nothing happened for the next three hours at the Luncheonette. The music had stopped. Outside, a late March snow fell. The two straw hatted figures remained in the same position. He watched the snowflakes, thinking of Celine. Here was that other Detroit. . . .

But Charles and Rosalie were kind people and, when time came to close, they offered him a ride. On the way, Charles remembered that a party of sorts was going on at somebody's place and Codrescu was invited.

The party was something else. In the room crowded with dancing, sweating black forms, drinking scotch and smoking pot, he lost, for a few minutes, all consciousness of who he was and why he was here . . . he didn't know why he was in America except, in a sense, he figured that an effort was underway to push him as far off his center as possible . . . to stretch his roots . . . but was there a pattern to all this or was he, like so many other exiles, wasting his time falling from one hallucination into another? That he entertained these kinds of thoughts was proof that, basically, he was still an old-fashioned soul yearning for a simple life . . . his shoes were falling apart . . . he didn't have a penny (twelve cents to be exact), he had, so far, trusted to the kindness of strangers . . . (not that they didn't owe him everything for being such a great poet!) . . . Well, he was a poet, and he had taken that to mean: Wits and Guts . . . Bigger and better states of otherworldliness! The only thing he regretted really was the sense of aesthetic order and place that Europe had . . . America was a wild place, without specific gravity. He could see, right there, the difficulty of being an American poet. Unlike a European, an American must invent an entire system of mytho-poetics, a whole world in order to ground himself . . . Walt Whitman's size was just the regular size American poets came in . . . But, of course, he was who he was and whatever that was, was what he was doing . . . ugh! He was blue.

Presently, his attention was captured by a most extraordinary scene: a fat man was facing him with a saxaphone in his mouth. He realized, with a start, that all he had taken for his thought poured out of the man's melancholy jazz and that furthermore, the man was actually reading his mind with the sax and suggesting the direction of his thoughts. The man was a wizard. He smiled. Everybody burst into laughter and applause. Later, Charles told him that the man, whose name was Dandolero, was a mind reader and that it had been nothing unusual for him to read a "keed's mind."

At the Wayne State University cafeteria, where he spent the endless day waiting for the concert that evening, he nursed an endless cup of coffee, writing in his diary . . . He spoke to a drifter, a mathematics student, a poet (an unfortunate victim of W.D. Snodgrass's middle-aged depression), two girls who were wanted by the police, a left-wing revolutionary whose politics were based on a Trotskyist pamphlet and a group of fraternity boys who were planning to set somebody on fire. What impressed him about all these people was their fantastic positivism. They were all filled with energy. They all believed in the immediate unfolding of the universe.

He was about to leave for the concert when an exceedingly familiar figure walked into the place. He recognized the long face with a shock. He knew it wasn't somebody he had met in America, in Europe, or even recently in Rumania. Who was this person? He shuffled his notebook over to the stranger's table and stared at him, open-mouthed. The stranger, upon seeing him, had the same kind of shock.

–Do I know you? he ventured in Rumanian.

162

–I have the same feeling, replied. . . .
–Berl!
–Andrei!

This was fantastic. His childhood friend, Berl, in this cafeteria, a million miles from Sibiu. They danced with delight. Berl lived with his father in a Jewish section of Detroit (his mother had died), and he was an engineering student at Wayne. They had been in America for ten years and Berl could barely speak Rumanian any more.

–I'm getting married, said Berl, to a Rumanian Jewish girl.

They went to a restaurant.
–What do you think of all these American hippies? said Berl.
–I'm afraid I'm one of them.
He then proceeded to tell the story of his departure, the story of his arrival, the story of his present circumstances.
–You're exactly the same, laughed Berl . . . You were like this in grammar school too. Be careful here though . . . these drugs and stuff will kill you and you'll end up in prison.

Talking, he had the distinct feeling that they were talking to each other over a chasm of years from two loudspeakers turned off somewhere in the past. Having arrived in America ten years before him, Berl had seen it all go from Elvis to the Doors, but had watched it from a distant, religious cell where he stayed rooted. Berl was a fervent Jew and there was an enviable solidity to his gestures, purposes, etc. Andrei was confused. They separated, after Berl invited him over the next day.
–My father will love to see you, he said. He always followed your family with a passion. He loved your father.

He lingered in the restaurant after Berl left. He felt that two ends of his life had been joined at this point for some inexplicable purpose. He had been in the process of becoming someone entirely different (his dream) when Berl walked in, breezily, reminding him of something he had forgotten. But what did he forget?

163

He felt like a chameleon surprised between two color changes. What did it all mean?

He missed the concert and, with it, his first public appearance in the New World.

23

Leslie had gone hitchhiking across the continent so he was now alone with Jimmy and Mildred in the house of a thousand illusions. He was alone, that is, until one afternoon when the ceiling seemed to collapse. Wild shouts emerged from it. He rushed upstairs where there lived a vast commune. He walked in. In the room directly above his, a big woman, completely naked, was discharging a revolver into the floorboards.

–What are you doing? he said.
–Every bullet is a mirror, she said. When one of them touches you, you see your entire life before you. Unfortunately, these bullets are blind. Once, I shot many seeing one . . . She extended her hand. My name is Luz Christina Dolores Aguilar.
–Andrei Codrescu Ivanovitch Goldmutter.
–I am a Peruvian Poet. I was a *guerrillera* expelled from my country for machine-gunning a police station. I believe in magic and I have seen crows turning into men and herbs that can make you into a sheep.

All her speeches were marvelously definitive. Once she said:
– *Vivir a puñaladas como la luz* (To live on the edge of light like the knives).

–Would you help me look for crabs? she said. He sat down and for the next fifteen minutes he parted her pubic hair in search of the elusive creatures.
–Let's make love, he said.

165

—I only make love to women and to men with fifteen inch cocks.

Well. He steered the conversation to her future plans with the gun which made a horrible noise in his room, under hers.

Luz had an ageless, ancient face with fabulous deep witchy lines in it. She was beautiful.

—You can have this gun, she said. You are my brother. He took it.

—I will learn to drive a car, said Luz, and then I will drive it into the General Motors building at great speed.

A jazz, poetry and revolution newspaper appeared in Detroit. It was called *Guerrilla*. Luz wrote a long article about South America for the first issue. Andrei contributed some translations. He had, by now, heard a lot about Dracula and the nonexistence of Transylvania. "Where are you from?" went the riff. "From Transylvania." "I didn't know there was such a place." It seemed as if everybody in America loved Dracula. The name means simply "devil" and it is, perhaps, the devil that everybody loves, which is natural in a country where He is the last challenge. Or the last frontier.

His collection of totems grew. In addition to the gun he now had tons of poetry books, a column in a revolutionary newspaper, a job and a fair knowledge of American. But something was missing. He told all of this to Luz, who was loading a rifle in the nude . . . she knew many poets because she was a traveler and spoke six languages.

—The link is love, she said. You have to be in love to see why things fit together instead of collapsing like boiled cabbage. All the poets who are not in love project their selves through the medium of dead ambitions. See you in New York, she added. She left that day with a tall man carrying two suitcases full of matchbooks, a lifetime collection which, he said, would set the world on fire some day.

He was sad to see Luz go.

166

The visit to Berl's house was a disappointment. Berl's father had aged a lot, could barely talk, and could not stop talking about his long hair.

—Above all, he said, your father could shoot a Nazi with his hair perfectly groomed . . . I never saw him unshaven and, even in the days when a piece of soap cost a hundred dollars, he looked as clean as a rose. . . .

Berl gently steered the discussion to America, but the old man had no patience with that. He didn't live in America. He lived in a world of continuing correspondence with the past.

That night he dropped some acid. He was waiting for a bus to take him home. In his hand he had a copy of Ginsberg's *Howl*, which he had been reading out loud, noticing how the lines became distorted and vanished at some point down the street. Suddenly he felt, with the accuracy of acid, a fabulous feminine presence walking toward him. When she came closer, he saw that it was Lemon, not skinny Lemon of his early youth but the embodiment of what Lemon had grown into in his head. She walked easily. He insinuated himself in front of her and, with a gesture replete with flickering emotion, he read her the entire text of *Howl* under the neon light. She listened.

—I have two tickets, she said, to the Jimmy Cotton Blues Band.

And so, they went to a music club and a merger took place in which the girl incorporated him by means of a net of sounds and made him dance wildly the whole time. They spent a symbiotic night together.

Her name was Alice. Aptly named, she had led him through a maze of strange worlds to the yellow bed in the middle of her apartment. This bed, called the Yellow Submarine, swayed amidst a sea of colorful objects, paintings, unfinished sketches, Indian blankets and umbrellas. Her blue eyes seemed to skip right over the obvious things in the world to look upon some private enchantment. The Lost and Found counter at the university, where she worked, appropriately described her at that time. One moment she would be lost on a long private voyage, the next she

167

would reappear, fully present, holding his face in her hands, her short blonde hair suddenly luminous. Andrei brought her donuts at work and she gave him umbrellas. The Lost and Found was a magic world of umbrellas. Thousands of lost and unclaimed umbrellas covered the walls of the small room. The two of them would walk down Woodward Avenue, holding each other under a big yellow umbrella. After work they would sneak up the stairs to her apartment, past the insane Arab landlord who hid under the stairway with bags full of Turkish candies, and as soon as they were in, Alice would open the curtains and take out her paints. She painted his face and hers. At night, she would load a bag full of colors and, for hours, they would go through the drabness of Detroit painting symbols on houses, traffic signs and sidewalks. Exhausted, they would drag themselves back, laughing, and the world was like a rainbow.

One night they went out to paint an enormous comic strip on the sidewalks. It was called *The Adventures of the Rag*, and it was the story of a poor rag in a city full of cops and muggers. Each adventure occupied one square of sidewalk cement and the strip was already three blocks long when they came to a big intersection. The last square contained the rag's paranoia . . . the rag was eating a police car . . . At the appointed time for coincidence, a police car stopped. They were made to spread eagle on the hood of it and were frisked.
  —My six year old daughter gets the switch for doing things like this, said one cop, pointing at the rag.

As soon as they were freed, they began laughing and calling their strip: *What a Cop's Daughter Gets the Switch for* or *Pig Kid Stuff*. They went on with it, across the street, and ended it, gloriously, at the Detroit Museum of Art on the back of a copy of Rodin's *Thinker*, on which they wrote,

WHAT'S THIS PIG THINKING ABOUT?
THE TIME FOR REVOLUTION IS NOW!

Alas, they were prophetic. Detroit was on the edge of a flying bomb.

WE HAVE FOUND TREASON, ANARCHY, INSURREC-
TION, REVOLUTION AND EVERYTHING THAT
THREATENS THE SECURITY OF THE STATE MORE
COMPATIBLE WITH POETRY THAN THE SALE OF
LARGE QUANTITIES OF LARD TO A NATION OF PIGS
AND DOGS.

These words, from Breton's second *Surrealist Manifesto,* stood
now in place of:

COME ON, PEOPLE NOW, GET TOGETHER LOVE
ONE ANOTHER RIGHT NOW on the frontispiece of the
Artist's Workshop in Detroit.

–I'm so happy to see you, said Jimmy when they got to the
house.

–Just a visit. The mood has certainly changed, from love to
guns . . . The stations on the radio keep doing Jim Morrison's
"C'mon baby, light my fire!"

Jimmy looked slowly out the window. Then he was startled.

–There it is, he said.

They looked out. Great billows of smoke covered the sky with
enormous tongues of flames jutting sporadically. Detroit was
burning. The riots had started.

–What a time to return, said Jimmy.

–We have an instinct for it, said Andrei and opened the door.
Luz was standing there.

–Just in time, Alice said.

–I wouldn't miss it for anything, said Luz. I don't come to
watch, I come to assist.

The joy of the first two days was unmistakeable. Rednecks and
blacks, hitherto hateful of each other, joined together in the
looting . . . Throngs of people holding hams, radios and jackets,
met each other at street corners and laughed with the delighted
laughter of anarchy. Expensive bottles of liquor were dropped
from six stories up and little cognac rainbows hovered over everything . . . Color TV sets stood unattended on street corners
because they had been dropped or their owners had decided to
go back and get portable sets. . . .

169

They watched from the roof as the tanks came. They rolled slowly up Woodward Avenue as National Guardsmen and Army paratroopers looked for signs of life in the windows darkened by curfew. Sporadic sniper fire was heard. Machine-gun fire was regular. In front of the stores with their gaping window fronts, soldiers patrolled sternly. He watched it all, wishing he was watching it on TV in Rumania. But Luz loved it. She mumbled incantations in the nude, over a candle, and disappeared on mysterious errands.

The fourth day, the door to their apartment burst open and two unidentifiable soldiers with machine guns came in.

–Everybody on the floor, they said. They tore the place apart. They found no guns. Luckily. Luz wasn't there and she always carried her gun with her.

–What's this all about? said Alice, indignantly.

–Let's shoot these sonsofbitches, George, said the younger man.

–Neah, said George, Let the faggots squirm. When they left, Jimmy bolted the door. He was shaking like a leaf.

–Good thing they didn't find the dope.

–They were after guns, not dope, said Luz, walking out of a closet. She had been there all along.

–This is how my daily life was in Lima, she said. Nothing to worry about. There is always a good cop and a bad cop.

–No cop at all is best, said the Angel of Detroit, who was busy that week, counting hundreds of mysterious and unreported corpses.

Two days later, they stuck their thumbs out. Alice painted a pear on his forehead and a peach on hers. A car stopped. "New York," the man said. So, New York it was.

24

A life, any life, is not a very long time . . . and yet, it is filled with a lot more than is necessary, he thought as they rolled through Ohio. "A good time is to be had by all," said the rookie cop who had picked them up. He was being painfully hip. I wonder what he would think, thought Andrei, if he saw the gun at the bottom of my duffle bag. Most likely, he wouldn't flinch. It is natural to have guns. The rookie chewed his bubble gum, looked at Alice's legs and revealed his dreams:

–I want to fly a helicopter. Zoom! Then I'll get a swanky pad and get chicks in there. Bam!

Father, father, he thought, take off that ridiculous outfit . . . and that machine gun . . . it's not good for the baby!

As they crossed the George Washington Bridge into Manhattan, he was in a wild mood.

–Let's sing, he said. But since the only tune he knew was *The International*, he chanted the words and sang this to it:

> I am young and horrible and fabulous
> And New York is a rotten gracious peach
> And though my body is particular
> My mind is a public beach!

The rookie was confused.

They lived in Harlem with friends. The neighborhood was ecstatic. Codrescu felt great. They were in the sinister projects of which many things were said but, with the exception of drunks falling and junkies puking, things were peaceful. The consciousness of being white hadn't, as yet, hit him. Alice, however, was blonde and unmistakeably Wasp.

–I'm really an Indian, she said quietly.

–That's Christ and the twelve apostles, said Crazy Larry one day. Crazy Larry was asymmetrical. His sunglasses were tilted from the right to the left, his right pant leg was shorter than the left and he had stripes running from the right to the left across his body. He was tilted at a forty-five degree angle.

They were standing in front of the old courthouse on the Lower East Side, a damp old jail, and he was referring to Ted Berrigan who had just come out of the place with his twelve students. They followed the group to Gem Spa on the corner of 2nd Avenue and St. Marks Place. Ted remained there, as the group dispersed. He stood there for a long time, his red beard falling occasionally into the glass of chocolate egg-cream in his hand. Thousands of freaks passed by, rearranging their affairs as they walked. Andrei approached.

–Hello, he said, I'm on acid.

–Great, said Ted. Why don't you kill somebody. I always wondered how it felt.

Meanwhile, a group of *Motherfuckers* who had just appointed themselves cops of the neighborhood by writing on their foreheads, LSD (Lowereast Side Defense), approached, led by their indefatigable leader, Bing Mort.

–Kill *that* guy, said Ted.

FREE FOOD! FREE FOOD! TWO BLOCKS DOWN AT THE GRAVEYARD! shouted Bing Mort, in obvious reference to Ted's territory, the St. Mark's Church-in-the-Bowery where readings went on.

A curious crowd drifted over (There was always a spare crowd on warm nights on that corner). Seeing that his accidental humor had drawn followers, Bing quickly changed his pitch:

172

–THE FUCKING PIGS JUST BUSTED TWO RIGHTON FIGHTERS FOR THE PEOPLE IN OUR HOUSE AND THE CIA IS MURDERING BOLIVIA! LET'S SHOW THE MOTHERFUCKERS!

The crowd was ready. Bing produced a handful of firecrackers and exploded them on the pavement. The crowd grew larger. "TO THE WEST SIDE!" shouted Bing and, throwing a side glance at Ted, who smiled mysteriously, he led the group in a gallop across the street . . . setting trash cans on fire . . . attracting more and more followers . . . breaking windows . . . Soon they were out of sight as the police sirens of the Sixth Precinct could be heard wailing after the party. . . .

Ted bought the *New York Times,* another egg-cream soda and a huge candy bar.
    –How can you eat that? Andrei inquired, sincerely nauseated.
    –If it fits your mouth, it's natural, said Ted.

Crazy Larry, who had watched all this with evident emotion, pulled a little box from his pocket.
    –Touch it! he said. Whenever I find the truth, I let somebody touch it. My foreskin is in there.

Codrescu worked at the 8th Street Bookstore. Alice went to school across the street at the New York Studio School. The bookstore was, mostly on Friday nights, a fabulous anthology of lunatics and geniuses, gliding in and out of the bookshelves, transported by the essence of the Village as by a flying saucer.

Over his typing desk at home, in the incredible depths of the Lower East Side (they had moved), stood this injunction:

ANYBODY WHO DOESN'T HAVE
HIS OR HER OFFICE
AT THE EDGE OF THE UNIVERSE
IS OUT TO LUNCH

The edge of the universe, which could be seen from his window,

173

teemed with pushcarts, stoned Puerto Ricans, old Ukrainian ladies with strollers, speedfreaks running in complicated patterns
across the park, leaflet-givers, panhandlers, underage girls, flower
children with painted legs, etc.

His gun lay forgotten on the bottom of the suitcase. Alice painted
portraits of people who would soon die or inherit fortunes.

Leader VanDoren, editor of *Guerrilla*, appeared unexpectedly in
New York and stayed at their place for two weeks, He would get
up chanting in Cuban, arguing about Trotskyism and Surrealism
and fulminating at the noncommital nature of most writers
. . . Codrescu included (his politics were strictly royalist, his code
strictly medieval). VanDoren hated the aristocracy. Everything
VanDoren saw was counterrevolutionary.

The New York School of Poetry, VanDoren said, has to be politi-
cized. He had a plan. He was going to assassinate Kenneth Koch.
This amusing idea fit very well in the spirit of the times which
had seen money thrown from the balcony of the Stock Exchange,
a bra made to fit the breasts of the Statue of Liberty hung over
Wall Street, the Living Theater, etc. It was a blissful time in
which the danger and the humor of America were still in some
sort of precarious balance.

The assassination took place in the Church at Koch's reading. He
was reading from the pulpit, describing his desire to eat the
vocabulary . . . he had the audience hypnotized when VanDoren
(who was seven feet tall and wore Army fatigues) jumped on the
altar and, pointing the gun to Kenneth's distinguished head, said:
   –DEATH TO BOURGEOIS POETRY!
and fired the blanks.
   At that point, the rest of the plotters threw heaps of posters
in the air, covering the audience with sheets of paper. These read:
POETRY IS REVOLUTION! Under this caption was a photograph of Leroy Jones, handcuffed and bleeding.
   Kenneth Koch gestured feebly, postmortem, and startled himself by looking in a mirror. He was very white.

174

This is very refreshing, Andrei thought. He tried to imagine a feigned assassination of Mihai Benuiuc. God! It would shake Rumania. Dada is a pleasure.

Mercifully, VanDoren soon moved out and the tension eased and the rest of the "plans" went unfulfilled. One particularly gorgeous Dada idea had been to blow up (for real) the offices of the *New York Times*. We said "moved out" but what actually happened was that Alice, who was highly sensitized, took the Leader's gun and papers and threw them out the window onto a boy scout troop. And when VanDoren tried to hit her, she threw a bucket of yellow paint at him.

–One Dada chases another Dada down Gaga Street, she said, with her characteristic economy.

25

He noticed a discoloring of the natural universe. He had translated himself into American. Even his dreams, which Alice said were usually in foreign languages, started speaking American. He had a hard time remembering his native tongue. He gave an interview for Radio Free Europe in a savagely distorted version of his language. He could not, entirely, speak the new language, so he was suspended from a delicate impotence. English, he realized, is a language of separation in which the less is said, the better we feel. In Romance languages, a lot of talk communicates a lot of warmth. In American, a lot of talk communicates a lot of anxiety. His anxiety over all these questions resulted in the poems Anne Waldman published in the *World*.

He looked at all the poets for clues. What, in the beginning, had been a search for an explanation of America became America.

Ginsberg, John Weiners and Peter Orlovsky did their laundry under his window in the little corner laundromat. The park was full of poets. The bookstores were full of poets. Was Paris in the thirties like this? Sanders's *Peace Eye Bookstore* had reopened under a barrage of rocks from local kids who did, however, quiet down when Ginsberg began chanting Hare Krishna. Allen's mysterious powers of pacification were well known. Once, in a violent bar brawl with flying chairs, Allen made peace with his finger cymbals. Surrounded by mimeograph magazines Andrei closed his eyes and tried to hear something beyond the wall of America

176

which kept growing, impenetrable and mysterious, all around him. The headlines were horrible. Vietnam.

Andrei gave his first reading at the Church. He began by pulling his gun out of his coat, putting it on the lectern, and saying, "This is my first poem!" He implied through this a certain continuity with America, but the balance had already shifted. In the race between the Funny and the Dangerous, the Horrible had won. After the reading, he walked slowly home, pleased with himself. When he crossed the street to go to his building, two solid figures pushed him into a hallway, frisked him briskly, extracted the gun and promptly arrested him.

In the cell at "The Tombs," surrounded by junkies who were eating and selling their pockets (old junkies always let a drop fall in their pockets before shooting up), he thought about guns. He had a passion for them. His political beliefs were negligible. He was an aristocrat and a royalist. He longed for the return of the monarchies. He longed for the protection of the Court.

The Court was brief. He was out on $5,000 bail. This was managed with the help of a giant poetry reading, loans and helpful donations. There was a certain amount of chic to getting busted in those days.

Luz reappeared and came to the rescue. She was uncanny. Luz was a witch. Her brew consisted of trouble, revolution and theater. She was in Detroit for the riots, in Paris for the student revolt, in Chicago for the Democratic Convention, in New York to help him. Rising adrenaline attracted her like a radio signal.
   —You have to leave, she said, if you don't like jail. I know sixteen men and four women in jail. I keep in touch with them telepathically but it is very hard to cheer them up. They are in need of affection.

This he didn't do. He stayed for the trial. The arresting officer had disappeared. The case was dismissed. When the judge wanted to know where the man had gone, he was informed that he had left the Force. Sheer luck!

–No, said Luz, it is not luck. I have done it with one mirror, a bottle of shaving lotion and a dry martini in which I brewed amanita muscaria.

Thank you, Luz.

Soon after, their apartment was invaded by cockroaches. They came in streams under the door, mutated, undaunted, arrogant and endless. Outside, the street had also, suddenly, been flooded by endless throngs of cripples, psychopaths, sex maniacs and junkies.

–Let's go to Europe, Alice said.

This is when he discovered that his passport had been stolen. He had turned the apartment upside down looking for it. It wasn't anywhere. He sat, for a long time, on the floor, looking out through the barred window at the slimy yard filled with wash lines and garbage. This is the end of a certain line, he thought. He was thoroughly lost. Alice tried to console him. I know who you are, she said. Maybe, he replied, but I don't. When I was a child I knew who I was. When I became Maria Parfenie I knew. When I got my Persian passport I knew. When I met you I knew. Even yesterday I had a fair day. But now I don't. I am America, I don't exist any longer. This is you, she said and touched his nose. He took her in his arms. He loved her. She knew.

Well, part of him was in the many collaborations he had written with the poets he had met. All the poets he knew collaborated incessantly, obsessively, losing themselves in the new human combinations they invented. Surrounded by clouds of grass, his contemporaries, like the Surrealists before them, yielded their identities in favor of their creations. In addition to these parts of himself, Codrescu also made up new poets, all by himself. These poets, like Maria Parfenie, came from his spirit of contradiction. He made up a poet-mechanic, a revolutionary, a junkie, another woman, a jailed Puerto Rican, a mystical fascist. The jailed Puerto Rican, Julio Hernandez, made the rounds of admirers. Robert Bly

178

wanted to free him from jail. Codrescu confessed: Julio Hernandez does not exist. Bly was angry. The woman, Aurelia, was published in various magazines. People fell in love with her. She was sexy and beautiful. They came to the house asking for her. Are you Aurelia? they asked Alice. I am Alice, she said. Then he made up poems by Alice. People fell in love with her. Andrei felt that there was no end to his imagination. He could invent worlds. But he had lost his passport. And his courage almost left him.

It was a group lunch at Ratner's. A poet was saying to the editor of a well-known magazine:

–I met a lover of yours who described some of the amazing S&M trips you guys go through.

–Oh, please tell me what he said, please do, said the editor.

–Well, he said that you don't know who you are until you start to eat shit while being whipped with a leather strap at least seven inches wide . . . and that, as soon as you're whipped you start screaming: Now I know! Now I know!

A strawberry shortcake flew into the poet's face. The editor was angry.

Andrei hoped that he would soon recover his consciousness of self without having to resort to such drastic measures. But he felt very low. They were surrounded by violence. They were being robbed, mugged and pushed around. Alice acquired a knife. What a courageous girl, he thought. He didn't know if he could ever use a knife. And if he had, then what? Would he then know who he was?

He was walking up 8th Street when Dan Arch, who wrote a sex column for *Screw* magazine, accosted him.

–Do you know where I can get a gun? he said.

–No.

Dan's job consisted of picking up four new girls a week, making love to them and writing down (on paper) every detail of what had gone on. He screwed with one hand in his notebook. A few days later, he saw Dan in a state of extreme agitation walking up and down 8th Street. "Come with me," he said. They walked up the

179

stairs to his flat on MacDougal. Dan unlocked the door, invited him in. A weird scene was going on.

Two girls about thirteen years old were tied up to each end of the bed, to the bed posts, stark naked. They were crying, trying to get loose. Dan went to a back room and came back, trembling, holding a rifle.

–What the hell are you doing? shouted Andrei.

–I don't know, he said, loading two big cartridges into the gun.

–Let these girls go, Dan! Christ!

Andrei was shouting as he never had. He knew that he was capable of strangling the madman. Suddenly Dan dropped the rifle and began to cry. Andrei grabbed the gun, untied the girls and unlocked the door. The girls grabbed their clothes and bolted out.

–What's with you, man?

–I don't know, the sex poet said.

–Do you even know who the fuck you are?

–I don't know.

–What's your name?

–I don't know.

Meanwhile, at the Studio School where Alice was modeling to pay for her classes, a sculptor fell in love with her breasts. One day, the sculptor caught up with them on the street and said:

–I'm going to join the Hare Krishnas. . . .

–Why?

–Because I love your tits and I can't stop myself from . . . er . . . cutting them off. . . .

–Go join the Hare Krishnas, man, before I bash your head in, said Andrei.

He was full of rage. He was so angry he could have smashed up the whole street. He was angry. That's who he was. Mr. Angry No Passport.

–Do you know anybody who wants to go to California? said the German hippy in front of Gem Spa.

–Yes, said Alice.

So they packed up in record time and gave their place to a friend and piled into the car the German had rented from a drive-away agency. In the car, as they were leaving New York, he looked at his last day's mail. There was a letter from Paul Carroll of Big Table Publishing Company in Chicago telling him that he had won the Big Table Younger Poets Award for his book, *License to Carry a Gun.* Appropriately, *License to Carry a Gun* was composed of three different sections written by three of his creations. None of these imaginary poets needed a passport. Only he did.

–America, das ist ketchup, said Erhard, the German, pointing at something or other.

26

There was another news, of paramount importance. Alice was pregnant. He was going to be a father. St. Augustine, crossing the heavens the way they were crossing the continent, leaned out of his car window and repeated his famous line: *God sent an animal to earth to tell men that they are immortal, and this animal, either through stupidity or through forgetfulness, told them that they must die.* Of course. They didn't have to die. Nobody had to die. There was a new being around the corner. Would he/she need a passport?

And thus, the suggestion was made, as they drove on through the ungraspable immensity of America, that the imagination of the universe was indeed endless. A being more real than his father, than Maria Parfenie, than Andrei Codrescu, was about to appear. The stars were huge. For all the bright little cities they drove through, millions of miles of wilderness sat in complete darkness or bright sunlight, nursing bizarre creations. It was always night. It rained. Flowers grew out of rocks, there were seas on top of mountains, rivers came out nowhere. Savage canyon walls, carved by wind into zillions of faces, lavished their images on the three travelers.

Erhard, with his Germanic explorer sense, made fires, cooked everything and played the guitar. He'd lived alone in the jungles of Brazil and the night kept no secrets from him. His ambition was to get a covered wagon, two horses, two girls and a violin, and roam the country roads as a sideshow. He took endless photos and painted tiny watercolors. At restaurants in one-street towns, he would pour hot sauce and ketchup into everything he ate. Clear chicken soup became red. The owners of the places, who also owned the gas stations and the patrol car, shook their heads. The big American flags stapled to the walls in back of them were covered with splattered grease.

Alice was drawing her diary. White lizards, rocks, birds, gophers, but mostly animals she had managed to avoid running over when she drove. Having saved their lives, she felt that they became her totemic animals and she drew them.

–I will have them tatooed on, she said.

He would have loved to see her right then covered with colored pictures of gophers, birds, squirrels, turtles and snakes while the new human being, at the center of her body, pushed on for light. Her ambition was to settle in a beautiful place where she would never run out of colors to paint.

Electrical lines whizzed through the sky carrying unreal quantities of energy to the big cities. Their hum was like chalk screeching across a vast blackboard. Everything raced, and not because they were driving at ninety-plus, but because nothing wanted to stay where it was, nothing wanted to be left alone, everything wanted out of itself. Hills would chase the car for miles. It was, actually, his definite impression that the North American continent was hitchhiking.

–The continent is hungry, said Alice.

–Really, said Erhard, I think that bush is perfectly edible.

Two A.M. in Arizona is the center of the U.S. the way the Forum is the center of Rome. At this hour, in this place, they stopped the car to get some sodas at an automated coin bar in the desert. Two drunk cowboys, leaning on their guns, staggered into the place.

–You girls want to go for a ride?

–No, said Erhard, we are going to Brazil.

The nine-foot-tall one lunged forward. He was, fortunately, so drunk that he fell on his face. His buddy bent over him.

They made a hasty exit.

183

–This is wilder than Brazil, said Erhard. The cowboys and the truck drivers make the law. The truck drivers, in their prehistoric monsters, sped by in clouds of benzedrine and country music.

KEEP AMERICA CLEAN. CUT YOUR HAIR.
THIS IS THE LAND OF THE AVERAGE JOE.
OUR COWS ARE OUTSTANDING IN THE FIELD, and, by golly, there they were!

They composed a song for the Average Joe:

> The electric fan makes him feel guilty
> And the chair does too
> The sofa does nothing except
> Hold a dead yew
> But the stove smells like hair
> The window is unbearable
> He'll throw himself out of it
> Like a darling vegetable!
> But instead he'll do a flip and
> Throw himself against the wall
> The fridge slams on his rocks
> And his head becomes a hole

Then, suddenly, after long nights, the Sierras came out of the night and on the other side was California, a place as mythical to them as New York is to the Rumanians, as mythical as Transylvania. The mountains, capped by snow, suggested, by some reverse trick, the ocean. Tropical waters covered with fallen white bananas. The function of the landscape was to suggest its logical opposite. Prelude to Fantasy Land. Where Eva Braun is actually the mistress of Jesus Christ and the Napoleonic Wars are the Thousand Years of Peace. All is illusion.

–California, said Alice.

–I will be a father, said Andrei.

There was no doubt about it. A sudden abandoned gentleness appeared in the air.

–There are two kinds of folk, said Erhard, and some go someplace and some go nowhere.

184

He was quoting Lee Marvin in *Paint Your Wagon*, the only movie he'd ever seen.

California burst on them.

They picked up a hitchhiker and he said:

—Come to our moon feast . . . We're having a big feast for the last virgin moon before they send their man up. . . .

The feast, on the eve of the first moonshot, was a wild, stoned affair on a deserted Pacific beach. The moon was full, unaware of its imminent deflowering, the tide was low and hundreds of grunions were stranded on the beach. They fried and ate these, passing wine and joints back and forth. He wrote a poem.

—Did you notice, said Alice, how different time is here?

It was true. Time had disappeared. They were suspended. California had a feeling of . . . well, postmortem peace. It was as if it had already sunk into the ocean and only an illusion was left.

This was, unfortunately, only one illusion because, almost the next minute, they drove into Los Angeles. Freeways, taco joints and Lone Ranger hamburgers, copulated and conversed over their heads. Colonel Sanders stared defiantly into the blue eyes of the Doggy Diner dog. Giant puppets dominated the place. Nathaniel West was everywhere as Celine had been in Detroit. The Charles Manson trial was in its fifth week. The Manson Family was in court with crosses tattooed on their foreheads. The Codrescu family stayed in the Blue Heaven Motel not far from the courthouse.

—I have a brilliant idea, he told Alice.

—What?

—I'm going to paint a cross on my forehead and go out.

—Why?

—Because I can't help myself.

—Christ! said Alice, touching her belly lightly. He did. Manson had appeared in court that day with an unfolded newspaper headlined: NIXON SAYS MANSON GUILTY. The jury, who hadn't seen the news, was shocked. Andrei hitchhiked to Sunset Strip with his red magic-marker cross. Every time he got into a

185

car, the passengers looked at his forehead and a chilly silence followed.

–What is that for?

–For Charlie, you know.

On the Strip, two black men grabbed his arms.

–You in the Family? they asked.

–We are all in it, he replied.

But he was scared. He went into the bathroom at a gas station to wipe off the red cross. Yes, California was certainly the place for cosmic Dada. Rays of light came through the bathroom window. The place was completely innocent and totally perverse. People here did not even get killed for human reasons. They were executed ideologically, exotically, mystically. The daily neurosis of New York turned here into magnificent psychosis, megalomania and worship. He jumped from star to star on Hollywood Boulevard.

–How did it go?

–Well, my dear, it went just fine. The place fits me like a glove. He bent down and kissed her belly.

–We are leaving tomorrow.

27

San Francisco arranged itself around them like the pages of a tremendous antibible. It was a wicked town filled with the most marvelous Mediterranean air and suicidal fog. Alice's belly arranged itself around him like the flesh of a hospitable melon. Everything came in circles. Poets, of one manner or another, filled the bars, the parks and the jails, writing, it seemed, morbidly circular visions, interrupting their dreaming only to watch the shadows of palm trees circling the cars, bizarre processions, street fighting and round explosions. With so little interruption and so much dreaming, the food-stamp armies of the elect formed the last human frontier. Everything moved counterclockwise in San Francisco and what the Spanish had put into the land did not get out at the arrival of Colonel Sanders. On the contrary, it had grown in guerrilla fashion. There was an active sadness here that gripped one's roots, speaking to things above one's conscious head. An atavistic calm reigned. The palm trees dripped with melancholy, the sea overthrew all discoveries and the sky, always impossible-blue and tight-grey, was the lid of a coffin. Millions of people bred in imperfections came here looking for perfection, only to discover that their individuality grew suddenly dim and their whole bodies turned into casual outlines. Being in San Francisco was the literal geographic translation of the desire to be round, handsome and forever young. In addition to eternal life, the place seemed to promise a perfect, faultless, spotless way of death. A successful death. And the main Spanish contribution to the spirit of the place was an architecture of death, a style of death with all the trimmings: stucco houses with red tiled roofs, wrought

187

iron balconies, winding stairways, spectacular views and the indif-
ference of the elements, the absolute boredom of the majestic sky.
In this landscape, dreams and hallucinations were the only possible art form. A de facto surrealism was the local style. The poets
here had a strong and aristocratic distaste for reality in spite of
their claims. The dream reigned and its language was an international poetic idiom. Codrescu felt great comfort. He was instantly
welcome in this city. Alice's paintings grew larger and larger to
accommodate the new space and so did her belly. She could now
take baths and read books on her belly without getting them wet.
Andrei dreamt that he too was pregnant. He dreamt that inside
him there was a big empty bus driven by his father. The bus
stopped in little towns along the way and picked up various
people. These people were not real people. They were fictions he
had created. The bus stopped in a field of yellow flowers. Alice
was there. She got on. He woke up.

Welfare, that wonderful institution, kept a thick dossier on the
Codrescu family. For a miserable 156 dollars a month, he had to
answer over and over, the same questions: STATE NAME IN
FULL, WHAT DO YOU DO, WHAT HAVE YOU DONE,
WHAT ARE YOU GOING TO DO? This annoying insis-
tence on history wasn't the sole property of the Social Services
Department. Other agents appeared. FBI agents dropped by
casually to show him pictures of people he'd never seen in his
life. Chemical agents, disguised as pills, herbs and powders
lifted his body to other spheres. Writers' agents came from New
York. And over and above it all, the supreme irony of California. Irony, as in the face of Timothy Leary and Charles Manson being held in the same prison, looking at each other across
vast brain spaces; one a genius, the other a fundamentalist, and
between them they mirrored the history of the race in its truest
dialectical postures:
the thought and the translation
the thought and the translation
the thought and the translation

188

Tom Veitch, who got rapidly to the heart of such things, said:

—What's this shit about translation? The Japanese have seven ways of saying "thank you" and each one implies a certain degree of resentment. You can't even translate a few resentments into each other, leave alone a whole language. . . .

Yes. And yet. Andrei had read his poetry in Folsom Prison and meeting those imprisoned writers there, he knew that only one translation was possible: freedom. Tom, who was a novelist like Tolstoi, saw panoramic views and he believed in roots and shades of interpretation. Andrei on the other hand had no roots and believed in revelations. Translation is an instinct not an interrogation. Codrescu could no more stop translating than guns could stop shooting. He could see that the Welfare Department, the political barbed wire of his times, the revolutions, etc., all of these had a vested interest in impairing his will to translate. But contrary to their expectation, Alice carried inside her a fantastic translation. Codrescu had translated himself already into a version of America. His body had grown longer. His memory was a blur. His poetry, which was a translation of high moments, tended to take off into cycles, books, epics, movements. It tended to crystallize and translate itself. The will to translate small fish into vast whales possessed him. He was in the throes of a translation megalomania. From one language into another! From one place to another! From one to two! From two to zero! And this was the essence of what California did to one's calling; she lent it its megalomania. A murderer acquired a claim in heaven! A poet got the green light on translation!

They were living above Dolores Park and their rooms were flooded with light. Alice painted everything, putting all the light she could in her paintings. She was becoming very round and very full. She painted nature with real passion. She bought plants and she looked for hours at trees and bushes.

—I want to abstract the city completely. It's only interesting when it looks like a bush, she said. He had always been a city boy but now, for some reason, he too would have liked to be in the country, surrounded by leaves. The idea consumed both of them.

189

The city like his past began to look like the face of a big dead feeling to him and the brilliance of trees and water flooded his imagination.

They left San Francisco in search of the place.

28

The sun was sending an oblique light over the mountain, making him feel like a solid gold egg. He would have liked, if he could have gotten up, to write a thousand letters. He would send these, every which way into the past and into the future, to relatives, friends and acquaintances, all over the world. He would ask them to do him the honor of being in his autobiography. If they said YES, he would then ask: "What relation to me would you like to have?" Would you like to be my mother, my friend, my father, my pet dog, my teacher? And then, so as not to lose perspective of a certain reality, where one earns a living, he would also ask: "What relation to me do you actually have?" It is possible that not a single one of them had the same relation to him that he had to them. Or vice versa. And, finally, the last question would be: "What stories about me have you told, been told, invented?" And he wanted to hear them all, all those stories he had no memory of, because there, in the sum of those tales, a single conclusion lay in weight: himself.

If his mind was like this, his life was not. He was at ease. Sadly so, sweetly so. And his feet, which hung over the railing of his porch, felt warm. And his son, Lucian, who was using a baseball bat to squash a banana slug, was far away, at the end of the hill. And Alice, who was pulling weeds out of the garden, was light blue. This was life in the country in California and the trees were so tall their tiny faces ate clouds. There was a stream in the back of the house and he could hear it carrying off little specks of gold, all the specks of gold that the gold miners had missed. Only a few days ago, he had found a goldpan, a sieve and a pick in the stream. A snake was in the sieve.